FOODS FROM
FRANCE

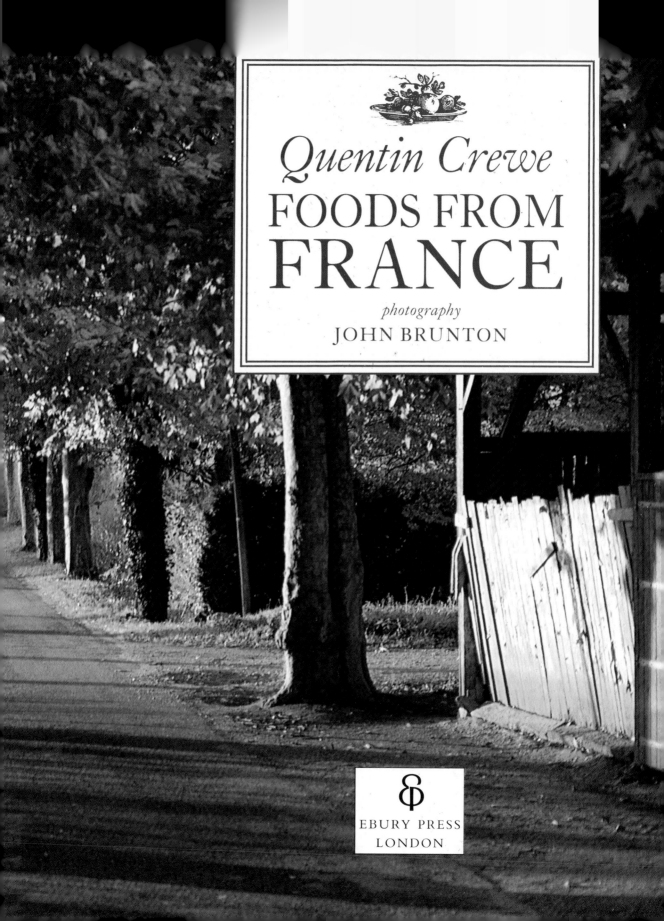

Quentin Crewe
FOODS FROM FRANCE

photography
JOHN BRUNTON

EBURY PRESS
LONDON

First published 1993

1 3 5 7 9 10 8 6 4 2

Copyright © Quentin Crewe and
John Brunton 1993

Quentin Crewe and John Brunton have
asserted their right to be identified as the
authors of this work.

First published in the United Kingdom in 1993 by
Ebury Press, Random House, 20 Vauxhall
Bridge Road, London SW1V 2SA

Random House Australia (Pty) Limited
20 Alfred Street, Milsons Point, Sydney
New South Wales 2061, Australia

Random House New Zealand Limited
18 Poland Road, Glenfield
Auckland 10, New Zealand

Random House South Africa (Pty) Limited
PO Box 337, Bergvlei, South Africa

Random House UK Limited Reg. No. 954009

A CIP catalogue record for this book is
available from the British Library.

Editor: *Susan Fleming*
Design: *Clive Hayball*
Maps: *Michael Hill*

ISBN 0 09 175289 2

Typeset by SX Composing Ltd, Rayleigh, Essex
Printed and bound in Italy by New Interlitho
S.p.a., Milan

Key to Map

1 Lamb 2 Oysters 3 Eels
4 Mushrooms 5 Foie Gras
6 Brebis Cheese 7 Armagnac
8 Cantal Cheese 9 Beef
10 Truffles 11 Vegetables
12 Olive Oil 13 Pigeons
14 Frogs 15 Poulets de Bresse
16 Char 17 Sancerre 18 Snails
19 Choucroute 20 Apples

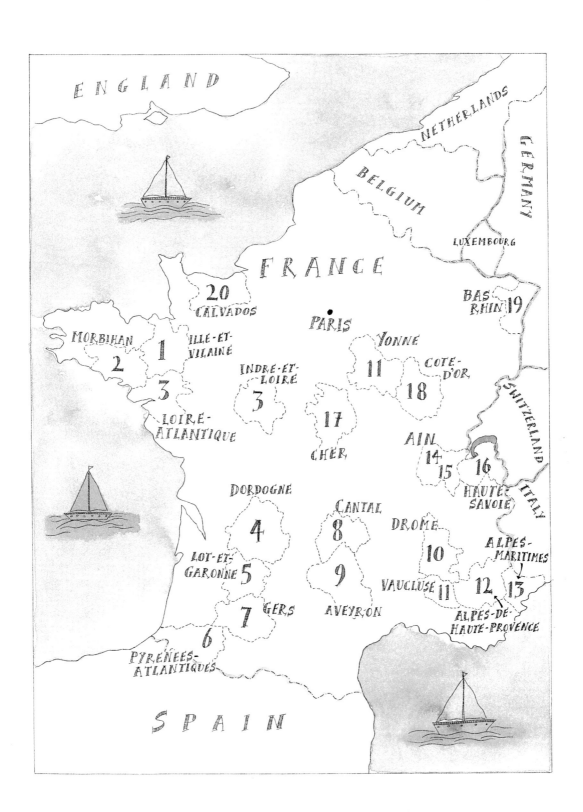

Quentin Crewe is a distinguished writer and traveller who has lived and worked in Britain, France, Italy and Japan. His travels have included an extraordinary journey crossing the Empty Quarter of Saudia Arabia (he was only the fourth European to do so) and a year-and-a-half trek through the Sahara. For some time he pursued a career in journalism and during the Sixties he was assistant editor of *Queen* and started his famous restaurant column.

Quentin Crewe has writen several other books, including *The Great Chefs of France, Touch the Happy Isles* and his autobiography, *Well, I Forget the Rest*. His writing has been described by Patrick Leigh Fermor as 'extremely perceptive and very entertaining'.

John Brunton has travelled widely throughout South-east Asia and Europe. From 1986 to 1990 he was based in Paris as correspondent for *You* magazine and he has also written and provided the photographs for feature articles for a wide range of publications such as English and Italian *Elle, Vogue* and the *Observer* magazine. In 1990 he travelled 8,000 miles around France photographing 'On The Waterfront' for the *Telegraph* magazine and he has published a book on Malaysia. He lives in Paris and New York.

Contents

INTRODUCTION	8		OLIVE OIL	86
LAMB	12		PIGEONS	92
OYSTERS	18		FROGS	100
EELS	24		POULETS DE BRESSE	108
MUSHROOMS	32		CHAR	116
FOIE GRAS	38		SANCERRE	124
BREBIS CHEESE	44		SNAILS	132
ARMAGNAC	50		CHOUCROUTE	140
CANTAL CHEESE	58		APPLES	148
BEEF	64		GAZETTEER	154
TRUFFLES	74		INDEX & ACKNOWLEDGEMENTS	158
VEGETABLES	80			

Introduction

It was John Brunton's idea that we should make this book. We had been working together on an article about Pierre Gleize and his son Jany, who run La Bonne Etape at Château-Arnoux, a restaurant of outstanding distinction.

The conversation at lunch had turned to the question of the fundamental importance of the quality of the ingredients used in *haute cuisine*, and from there to the vital role played by the growers, breeders and suppliers of those ingredients.

It so happened that several of Pierre and Jany's suppliers were interesting characters, usually working in old-fashioned and traditional ways, and it was plain that their relationship with the Gleizes was not simply a commercial one. They were established friends, whom they could trust, and whose objectives were the same as their own, which is to say the pursuit of quality.

It was Pierre who found Madame Dillard, who supplies not only him with pigeons, but several other restaurateurs of high standing, on the strength of his recommendation. 'I will always tell my friends of a good new supplier. It is not right to keep them secret, we are all trying to achieve the same degree of excellence.' At the same time, Pierre is quite strict with his suppliers. He warns them that if their standards drop, because of over-production for example, he will not hesitate to make a change and will advise all his friends to do the same.

At the end of this happy lunch, John said, 'Why don't we do a book about suppliers? They are, after all, the very foundation on which French cuisine is built.'

The idea was to settle on a list of ingredients and discover who cooked each one to the best advantage and then to find out who supplied him with whatever it was. The compiling of the list was difficult. Too many would become repetitive, but what could we eliminate? The ways of fishermen are, on the whole, similar the world over. It did not seem to us that the French had any particular way of catching sea-bass or *rouget*, so we left out fish from the sea.

Sometimes the obvious proved true: there is no better chicken than a *poulet de Bresse*. At other times it was false. We had assumed that Charolais would be the beef to choose. We soon discovered that most chefs of the top class think little of it; its taste has gone, a victim of ignorant consumer pressure. Ducks might well have earned a place in our list, but they would have borne too close a resemblance to *foie gras*. And how could we choose between France's 300 and more cheeses? We plumped for two being produced in a traditional manner: even so we have no goat's cheese, though *crottin de Chavignol* gets a nod in another context.

Wine and spirits presented a similar problem, which we resolved in an arbitrary, personal fashion. Sancerre is plainly not the finest French wine, but John is a *Chevalier de Sancerre* and I am a *Mousquetaire*, pledged to promote Armagnac, which I therefore maintain is the best *eau-de-vie* in France.

There are, of course, other important ingredients in French cooking that did not lend themselves to our theme, such as butter or even salt, which one meticulous restaurateur urged us to consider. Our choice was governed, too, by a wish to cover as many different areas of the country as possible. So it was that we started on an extremely agreeable tour of France, eating too much and learning many surprising things along the way.

As far as the traditional crafts and methods of production go, the picture is not an altogether happy one. Commercialisation threatens the quality of produce alarmingly. In a different way, the regulations imposed by the EC make it impossible for small producers to follow their time-honoured ways of doing things. Cantal cheese is a perfect example of this: factory-made Cantal is a drab thing; real Cantal, a subtle delight, has virtually ceased to exist.

Against that, on the gastronomic and restaurant front, I found much that was very encouraging. Thirteen years ago, I wrote a book entitled *The Great Chefs of France*. It celebrated what seemed to me to be the liberation of French cooking from the straitjacket imposed on it at the beginning of the century by Escoffier, the famous chef of the Savoy and the Ritz.

The bulk of the book was concerned with eleven chef-patrons who followed the example of Fernand Point. This most illustrious chef of the 1930s and 1940s was apparently the first to notice that *haute cuisine* had become so wrapped up in its sauces that the taste of the ingredients was lost, and also that times and customs were changing.

I included a few highly independent characters: Raymond Thuilier, whose restaurant was then one of the few examples of unfailing good taste in other things as well as the food; Charles Barrier, a philosopher of a chef who one feels has been there for 100 years; Jacques Pic of Valence, the most engaging of men, who pursued excellence without any reference to what anyone else was doing. One of these, Barrier, and Pic's son, with their respect for traditions, happily find a place in this book as well. The rest of them were a closely-knit group, who took much of their inspiration from Paul Bocuse of Collonge Mont d'Or, just outside Lyon. They were known as the *Bande à Bocuse*, which caused M. Thuilier to make ribald jokes, '*bande*' in French having more than one meaning.

Bocuse did much for the standing of chefs. At about the time my book came out, they suddenly became media stars – Vergé, Outhier, Guérard, Troisgros and all. Bocuse was given the Legion of Honour. He and his friends started to dash round the world, cooking meals in Australia one week and America the next. They became consultants in the Far East; Bocuse even opened a cookery school in Japan.

I was proud of the book at the time, with its fine photographs by Anthony Blake. Now, I am rather thankful that it is out of print. The whole heady rush of glamour of which it was a reflection was in the end, I believe, very damaging to French cookery and to France's restaurants.

The glorification of chefs led to several problems. First, because of their trips abroad, the grand chefs were absent from their kitchens for long periods. Anyone who has ever had anything to do with a restaurant knows that really high standards can only be maintained by the constant vigilance of the person who set those standards in the first place.

The next ill-effect was that any young man who had worked for two short years in one of the famous kitchens could find a backer, who would set him up in a restaurant of his own. The young man, usually, would be able only to produce indifferent copies of what his employer had done. He would have no real mastery of the essential fundamentals. This, coupled with all the publicity, meant that bad restaurants sprang up all over France, serving exactly the same food with no regard for regional differences. For a long time, it was impossible to escape from Bocuse's truffle soup and the Troisgros brothers' salmon with sorrel.

Possibly the worst effect of the general brouhaha was the air of commercialism that spread among grand restaurants. Instead of being shrines of gastronomy, admittedly a little holier than thou, they became big businesses. I cannot help feeling that the *Guide Michelin* was partly instrumental in this, because they appeared for a time to give their highest awards to places that spent a lot of money on decoration and fancy frippery. Restaurateurs striving for their third star, which can increase the turnover by as much as 60 per cent, took to borrowing enormous sums. Bernard Loiseau, the latest three-star chef, is said to have borrowed five million dollars. He is a superb chef of complete integrity but, with interest to pay on that sort of money, it would not be surprising in other cases if the need for cash took the place of dedication to quality as the primary spur.

Bocuse himself, always an enthusiast for marketing, has betrayed everything that he originally stood for, in my view, by selling vacuum-packed food and pretending in television advertisements that it tastes just the same as fresh food from his kitchens. This from a man who has spent hours telling me about the sanctity of ingredients and the importance of a living flame to cook over.

Pierre and Jany Gleize with their fruit supplier. The relationship between the chefs and their fournisseurs
*is one of friendship and trust. The suppliers do not use the back door, but will often come into the bar and
sit among the customers having a glass of wine.*

I had become depressed by all this and feared for the future. But, in the course
of our journeys all over France, I discovered that there was a new spirit abroad and,
in a great many places, a complete swing away from everything I had come to
dread. There is a number of young chefs to whom the flash, media-conscious behaviour of the chefs of the late 1970s and 1980s is anathema. They are not in any
sense a group, but they share a determination to get back to essentials and to the
regional traditions, laying much emphasis on the use of local products.

You will meet several of them in this volume, but there are many more. Just as
Pierre and Jany Gleize, the true inspirers of this book, have run the most faithfully
excellent Provençal restaurant that exists, this new breed of chefs will do the same
for their regions. In the hands of such people, who care so much for their *terroir* and
for their craft, I feel that the future of French cuisine is safe once again.

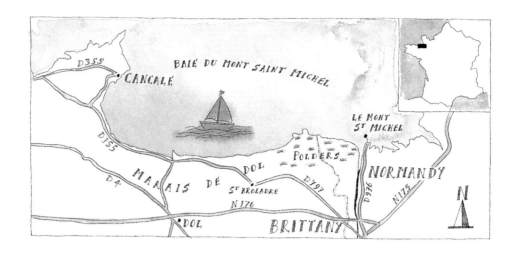

Lamb

The different provinces of France are quite chauvinistic about the lambs of their region. My friend Pierre Gleize (see Introduction and the piece on olive oil) asked me which area we had chosen for lamb. He pretended indignation when I said the borders of Normandy and Brittany, where the lambs known as *pré-salé* come from.

'What is the matter with the Alpine lambs of Sisteron?' he wanted to know. 'They are the best.' Of course, there is nothing the matter with them, and Pierre cooks them beautifully. He insisted that we should go to see one of the farmers from whom he gets his lambs.

Raymond Boyer lives in a crumbling hamlet, beside a derelict chapel. The farm lies in the foothills of the high alps, the green, close-cropped pastures rising steeply between clumps of oak. It has a lost feeling, as if belonging to another time. A donkey and some goats scrounge around. It is untidy, but there are signs of an attempt to make it pretty – a few roses, some cherry trees, a chestnut, the pink shower of a tamarisk and, least expected of all, a golden pheasant pecking about for scraps. Apart from a few forgotten, rusty cars, the farm might just as well belong to the last century although, round a bend in the track leading to it, one can see modernity in the shape of a dam in the Durance River, and a row of pylons striding off towards Aix or Marseille.

Boyer keeps 220 ewes and three rams. For the greater part of the year they browse over the 200 hectares (500 acres) of his pastures, eating the wild Provençal herbs that give the lambs the special flavour that Pierre is so proud of. For the two cold months of winter, he brings them indoors and feeds them on a mixture of maize and lucerne. But, as soon as it is warm enough, he puts them out again and the lambs grow strong on the rough mountain grazing.

To the lay eye, his sheep look rather scrawny, certainly not the fluffy, cuddly creatures of nursery rhymes. They are bred not for their wool, but for their meat, which dictates their shape – gangly legs for the *gigot* and a long back for the *selle d'agneau*. The lambs take between 125 and 150 days to reach the ideal weight for slaughter, which is to say 30–35 kg (66–77 lb), the carcass weighing about half that.

Pierre made us a superb *carré d'agneau* to convince us, but we were adamant. 'Never mind,' he said, 'you have that other kind of animal. For me, I wouldn't know how to cook it.'

So it was that we found ourselves at Cancale, where Olivier Roellinger knows better than anyone how to cook a *pré-salé* lamb. The fishing port of Cancale sits on the north shore of Brittany at the western end of a wide bay, a few miles from St Malo. On a clear day one can discern, in the distance, across the border in Normandy, the romantic shape of Mont St Michel.

Olivier is one of the finest of the new young generation of chefs, dedicated to the idea of reviving the regional nature of French cooking by using the produce of

For centuries Mont St Michel has watched over the salty grasslands where the sturdy pré-salé *lambs graze. Every day the flocks walk out to the strip of land beyond the dykes.*

the area they work in. He is unusual in that his family had no connection before with cookery or hotel-keeping, but he was from childhood determined to be a chef. Now he owns a Michelin two-star restaurant, the Maison de Bricourt, and, in association with it, a small hotel overlooking the sea.

The restaurant is in the middle of the town of Cancale, in what was the family home where he was born. It is a beautiful old house, originally belonging to a family associated with the Compagnie des Indes (the French equivalent of the English East India Company), which had its seat in St Malo. This connection with both the house and the region has been an important factor in Olivier's cuisine, in which he makes amazing use of a huge variety of spices. Quite apart from the fish and the shellfish and, as we shall see, the *pré-salé* lamb, which are the natural produce of the area, there is a strong tradition of spices here, for they used to pour into St Malo from the East.

'It was the search for spices that prompted the exploration of the world by Europeans. It was a grand adventure and this is my inspiration. . . . Here, I have such wonderful produce and I like to do something adventurous with it. To hell with caviar, I want to work with what comes from round here – all the seafood, the lambs, even the potatoes that I know, for example.'

The land around is in some ways odd. Inland there is hilly country, known locally as *le terrain*, nourished by several rivers but with a thin, stony soil not very good for agriculture. Nearer to the sea, the land drops abruptly and there is a wide flat strip of what was once marsh. There are traces of seventh-century fishing villages near the old shoreline. But the tides surged in and mingled with the floodwaters of the inland rivers so that, in the Middle Ages, the marsh was known for its dank, unhealthy mists.

In the sixteenth century came the first attempts to hold back the sea and let out the pluvial waters from the land. A dyke, known as the dyke of Duchesse Anne, was raised and still today forms a part of the elaborate system of dykes that allows the old marshland to grow crops (for some reason predominantly carrots, known as *carottes de sable*). There is still a small, sixteenth-century, grey stone chapel dedicated to St Anne standing alone, near to where the sea was first restrained by the Duchesse Anne dyke, and one can see on hillocks, in what now appears to be dry land, the old moorings of the fishing boats of that time.

The Compagnie Polder was formed, and in the mid nineteenth century Napoleon III gave it the right to reclaim some further 3,000 hectares (7,500 acres) of land, by the building of more dykes and the controlling of the capricious rivers that kept changing course. With the help of Dutch experts, the present-day pattern of dykes and the modern shoreline were established. ('Polder' is a word from Dutch meaning a piece of low-lying land reclaimed from sea, lake or river, and protected by dykes.) The result of the Compagnie Polder's enterprise was a most peculiar agricultural development. The company built a series of nearly identical,

The farmhouses of the Compagnie Polder have a Dutch solidity and spaciousness and, unexpectedly, many people from Holland spend their holidays on this coast with its land reclaimed from the sea.

spacious farmhouses in the local grey-brown stone, more Dutch in style than French, and allotted to each of them 100 hectares (250 acres).

Between the last of the dykes and the sea is a strip of grassland liable to be flooded, especially by the high equinoctial tides, and it is on this strip, known as the *herbus*, that the famous *pré-salé* lambs graze.

Yves Fantou is a butcher whose family business in the village of St-Broladre has been established for nearly 100 years. He specialises in *pré-salé* lamb and supplies Olivier Roellinger with the meat for his magical *carré d'agneau* with the kidneys attached and a delicious crisp skin.

Yves' uncle and aunt live in one of the Compagnie Polder houses and he took us to meet them. In quite a different way from our visit to Raymond Boyer, this was again like stepping back into the last century. Here everything was perfectly preserved and I had the feeling of having wandered into a story by Flaubert. The large room in which we sat was filled with immense pieces of nineteenth-century furniture. The old lady was proud of each one of them. 'That is our great-grandmother's buffet and this cupboard belonged to our grandfather.' In the middle of the room was a long table which could easily have seated sixteen people. The whole place spoke of more prosperous days.

The special grazing, and the long walks the wiry pré-salé lambs undertake, combine to give their meat its particular flavour and texture.

The old people keep a flock of 500 sheep. Every day the flock walks out to the strip of grass beyond the dykes, which in the case of many farms may be as far as 4 km (2½ miles). There they graze on the salt sea-grass, avoiding the *salicorne*, or samphire, and it is a combination of this and the long walks that give the lambs their particular flavour and texture. The only time when they do not go to graze by the shore is after a high tide has flooded these sea pastures. Then they must wait for a fortnight or until it rains enough to wash the grass.

Yves' uncle and aunt spoke of when they had their own shepherds, but today this is not economically possible. No-one will work the long, lonely hours nor sleep on the farmhouse floor as they used to. Now, most of the farmers share the services of a shepherd or, more often, use their children to guard the sheep.

'It was a hard life for the shepherds,' said Yves, who has often watched over his family's flocks, 'but you would be surprised how quickly the time passes and some of them do other things at the same time. I knew one who was a talented sculptor.'

The economics of a *pré-salé* flock are tricky. With an ordinary flock of sheep, a farmer can expect to sell 1.6 lambs for every ewe, but with *pré-salé* sheep the figure is only 0.8 lambs per ewe, exactly half. The long walks out to the grazing and back take their toll, killing many lambs. Then the Domaine Maritime levy a tax on every ewe.

For *pré-salé* lamb in his butcher's shop, Yves has to charge roughly twice the price of ordinary lamb. Needless to say, this discrepancy leads to a lot of cheating. Much lamb sold as *pré-salé* is nothing of the sort, but Yves and the genuine farmers are agitating for an *appellation contrôlée*, which would ensure that the lambs were genuinely fed on the shoreline grasses.

The question is, how does this lamb compare with other lambs? It is easy, once one has tasted it, to understand Pierre Gleize's point. It is a completely different animal. The meat is darker, not so tender and having a flavour almost of game. In Olivier Roellinger's care, it is a glorious new experience. In the end, however, it must come down to a question of personal taste or, of course, of chauvinism.

Petits homards aux saveurs de l'Ile aux Epices

SPICY LITTLE LOBSTERS

For 4
2 lobsters, about 500 g (18 oz) each
½ unripe mango, peeled and finely sliced
4-8 young lettuce leaves
about 100 g (4 oz) raw sprouts (see page 72)
Sauce
a dash of olive oil
50 g (2 oz) fresh ginger, peeled and shredded
30 g (1¼ oz) fresh galangal, peeled and shredded
1 garlic clove, peeled and blanched
10 g (¼ oz) allspice berries
5 mm (¼ in) vanilla pod
a pinch of ground mace
¼ whole nutmeg, grated
10 little white mushrooms, finely chopped
20 g (¾ oz) tamarind paste
5 lime leaves (or fresh coriander leaves)
juice of 1 lime
50 g (2 oz) butter

For the sauce, heat the olive oil in a large saucepan, and gently fry the ginger, galangal, garlic, allspice berries, vanilla, mace and nutmeg. Cook for 2 minutes, then add the mushrooms. Add 500 ml (17 fl oz) water, then the tamarind paste. Cover and simmer for 30 minutes. Strain, discarding the spices.

Cook the lobsters in the sauce for 10 minutes. Cut them in half lengthwise; remove stomach and intestinal tract.

Add the lime leaves and lime juice to the sauce, then beat in the butter. Strain again.

Arrange on each plate a half lobster, with slices of mango on the lettuce leaves. Coat with the sauce, and decorate with sprouts.

Most of the spices used in these two recipes can be found in Indian grocers. *Greater galangal* is the spicy root of a member of the ginger family; *lesser galangal* is a peppery gingery rhizome. They may be found fresh or dried.

Rond de selle d'agneau de pré-salé du Mont St Michel

ROLLED SADDLE OF SALT-MEADOW LAMB

For 4
½ saddle of lamb, about 1.5 kg (3-3½ lb)
1 fresh lamb's kidney
50 g (2 oz) butter
2 sprigs of fresh mint, finely chopped
Spices
1 teaspoon each of the following seeds: green cardamom, cumin, coriander, sesame, nigella or *quatre épices*, black pepper or grains of paradise
To serve
1 cucumber
8 spinach leaves
225 g (8 oz) small French beans, trimmed

Preheat the oven to 240°C(475°F) Gas 9.

Bone the meat carefully. Place the kidney on top of the meat.

Grind the seeds in a grinder or mortar, and sprinkle most of them over the meat.

Roll the meat around the kidney, and tie up with string. Roast in the preheated oven for 15 minutes for rare (a little longer for medium). Remove and keep it warm.

Meanwhile prepare the accompaniments. Peel the cucumber, slice in half, and seed. Salt lightly and leave to drain. Purée in a blender. Wash and drain the spinach. Cook the beans lightly in 30 g (1¼ oz) of the butter.

Add enough water to the roasting juices to make a sauce. Add a little of the spice mixture, the remaining butter and the mint.

Slice the meat, and coat with the sauce. Serve with the cold cucumber purée, the raw spinach and the warm buttery beans.

Olivier Roellinger

Nigella seeds come from a type of love-in-the-mist flower. In France, they are sometimes known as *quatre-épices*.
Grains of paradise are the seeds of a plant related to cardamom, and are very peppery.

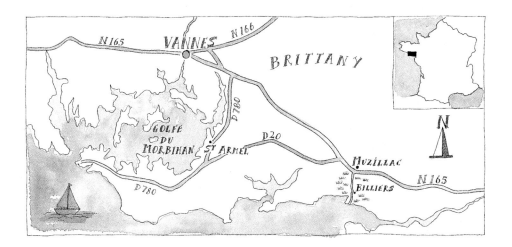

Oysters

Oysters all over the world have different associations. In England, in the last century, they were regarded as a dish for the poor, in the way that winkles and whelks still are. Nowadays, they are thought of as a luxury. In Japan, where raw fish is esteemed, oysters are thought very commonplace, definitely not something one would offer to a guest. In France, oysters have a strong association with Christmas, and at that time supermarkets all over the country, even miles from the sea, have a large selection – Belons, *fines de claires, fines de claires spéciales*. Belons are flat shelled, like English or Irish oysters, but the others, known as *creuses*, are longer, deeper and tinged with a little green.

The Golfe de Morbihan on the Atlantic coast of Brittany is like an inland sea, dotted with as many islands as there are days of the year. It is a peaceful place, calmer than the rest of the rocky coast. The villages round its shore are simple and quiet, populated by fishermen. Just outside St Armel, Michel Haumont lives in a caravan amid a series of small rectangular ponds. Even by the standards of French peasant smallholdings, his 10 hectares (25 acres) and the half-finished buildings by his caravan are a higgledy-piggledy mess. He himself is a stocky, red-faced man in his late forties, a twinkly, voluble character of decidedly eccentric manner. Yet Michel is one of the most superior cultivators of oysters in the province.

I use the word 'cultivator', because Michel does not breed them. In fact, when I asked him about the mating arrangements of oysters, he said he had no idea what they did, as it did not concern him in any way.

In fact, oysters breed in one of two rather chancy ways, depending on their variety, complicated by the confusing arrangement by which all oysters change

Michel Aumont believes in allowing his oysters a more natural life in the sea, whereas most cultivators enclose them in baskets. He gives them liberty even at the risk of losing some.

their sex at least once during their lifetime. In the first method, the male releases its sperm into the sea and the female sucks it up. As soon as the larvae develop, she ejects them again back into the sea where the oysters develop on their own, usually clinging to a rock.

In the alternative method, the male releases its sperm as before and thus, with luck, fertilises eggs similarly released by the female.

Oysters that are getting ready to spawn, usually in the summer months, become unpleasantly milky, which is why we do not eat them at this time, nor immediately after they have spawned, when they are small and thin.

The raising of oysters is a lengthy business. Michel gathers his baby oysters from the sea and then puts them into what you might call a park with its own boundaries, reserved for him. Most cultivators put their oysters in special pockets so that they cannot move or, rather, be moved by the tides and the currents. Michel believes that they grow better and larger if they are left free to take their chance in a more natural way. They stay two to three years in the sea park, living off plankton, and are then brought into the rectangular ponds, known as *claires*. Here Michel keeps them in flat wire baskets, which he calls *poches*.

What may look to be a muddle is, in fact, an extremely complicated system of

Left: *In France, oysters are not the rarity that they are in Britain. At Christmas, even the supermarkets have abundant supplies.* Right: *The wild Brittany coast is in strict contrast to the comforts of this luxurious hotel.*

irrigation, created entirely by Michel. The *claires* are fed with constantly changing sea water and, in these ponds, the oysters develop for another two or three years. Being kept in this controlled environment, instead of the hurly-burly of the sea, ensures that the oysters are cleaner and lose much of the greeny colour that a wild oyster acquires.

Michel walked us down a new road that he had made, as part of a sea-retaining wall, to the river where he gathers mussels. On the way, we passed sixteen or more old Citroëns, mostly derelict. He explained that he liked Citroëns for their suspension, which meant that he could raise them right up and back them into the water to load his shellfish.

But what he really wanted to do was to get back to his oysters, '*mes enfants*', as he called them. So we settled down by the *claires* and Michel brought a bottle of Touraine wine and then hauled out a *poche* from one of the *claires* and started to open some oysters. He does occasionally have some Belons, which he explained is no longer an *appellation contrôlée*, but he opened for us some *fines de claires spéciales* – the *spéciales* means fewer oysters are kept in a *claire* so they grow bigger.

Michel produces about 250 kg (550 lb) a year of his fine oysters, which is to say roughly 2,000. He markets his other shellfish under the name 'Rhuys Coquillage', but the oysters sell by the grand name of 'Comtesse de Moncial'. As his production is small, it is mostly consumed locally, but Michel says that there is nothing to worry about if oysters come from a long way away. Chilled, they stay alive for at least ten days and can survive for up to a month.

We, on the other hand, did not wait. Michel plucked out another *poche*. It was only ten-thirty in the morning, but it was soon time for another bottle of wine, and another and more oysters and then another. I can think of no pleasanter way to spend a sunny autumn morning, eating oysters by the Golfe de Morbihan and drinking wine in the company of this merry character.

It was Patrice Caillault, the chef at the Domaine du Château de Rochevilaine at Billiers, near Muzillac, half an hour south of the Golfe, who had told us about

The purists maintain that oysters are better raw than cooked. The practice of adding vinegar and hot spices is a relic of the days when the Romans used to ship oysters from Britain and northern France to Italy, and had to preserve them.

Michel. 'For our standards we have to have something distinctive, and here is this man who lives for nothing except his oysters. He looks only for quality.'

The Domaine du Château de Rochevilaine is itself an oddity. The hotel is a conglomeration of buildings, each in a different Breton style. It sits at the end of a rocky promontory that juts out into a threatening and angry sea. At times a mist descends and the beam of the lighthouse peers dimly into the murk. The place was built by an eccentric, who was enchanted by the situation and wanted to make a kind of record of the local architecture. It was bought by a group of doctors with a view to making it into a therapy centre. Somehow the centre never seems to get under way and, meanwhile, Patrice and his wife run the place as a hotel.

Patrice, who comes from Touraine, is passionate about using local produce. 'We have, naturally the best possible fish, good meat and,' he adds rather esoterically, 'the best salt in France.' This last comes from the slightly eerie salt marshes at the mouth of the Vilaine. 'The only things we lack are game and wine,' although, funnily enough, I did see a pheasant on the road not far away.

Patrice admits that all oysters are really better eaten raw but, if you are going to cook them, the *creuses* are better than the flat ones.

He could have listed the lobsters of the region among the delights of his area. In his hands they are superb, made into two courses, with the body roasted and the claws poached with vegetables. In April and May, he is proudest of his langoustines, marinated in olive oil and lime juice with fennel, and served in halves on a bed of *tomates concassés*.

Brittany has never seemed to me one of the more interesting parts of France, but these two men went a long way towards changing my mind.

Cromesquis d'huîtres aux poireaux

DEEP-FRIED JELLIED OYSTERS WITH LEEKS

For 4
3 dozen oysters
4 leeks
200 ml (7 fl oz) double cream
2 tarragon leaves
5 leaves of gelatine, soaked in cold water to soften
plain flour
1 egg, beaten
breadcrumbs
peanut oil for deep-frying
50 g (2 oz) butter

Open the oysters carefully, and keep their juices. Discard the shells.

Cut the leeks lengthwise, clean and chop them finely. Blanch them in boiling water, drain well, then simmer in the cream with the tarragon. When cooked put into the blender and purée.

While still hot, add the soaked gelatine and stir well to mix. Pour on to a baking sheet coated with clingfilm, and smooth out to 1 cm (½ in) thick. Dot the oysters regularly over the leek purée, pressing them in slightly, then chill in the fridge to set.

Cut the oyster-dotted jelly in order to obtain cubes with one oyster in each. Roll in the flour, then in the beaten egg, then in the breadcrumbs. Do this twice. Heat the oil, then deep-fry the *cromesquis* until light golden. Drain on absorbent paper and serve with the oyster juices beaten into the melted butter.

Petits feuilletés d'huîtres au seigle

OYSTERS IN PUFF PASTRY WITH RYE

For 4
3 dozen oysters
300 g (11 oz) puff pastry
25 g (1 oz) rye grains, roughly ground
150 ml (5 fl oz) Coteaux du Layon wine (dry white)
50 g (2 oz) smoked breast of goose, diced
100 g (4 oz) butter
200 g (7 oz) spinach leaves, blanched
1 bunch of chervil, finely cut

Preheat the oven to 220° (425°) Gas 7.

Roll the pastry out on a lightly floured surface to 3 mm (⅛ in) thick. Sprinkle with the rye. Cut into little circles, about 6-9 cm (2½-3½ in) in diameter, and arrange on a baking sheet. Bake for 10 minutes or until puffed and golden. Remove and keep warm.

In the meantime, open the oysters carefully, keeping their juices. Discard the shells.

In a saucepan, boil the white wine with the goose meat dice to reduce by half. Poach the oysters in their juices – moments only – then strain the juices into the pan with the wine. Beat the butter into this.

Cut the pastry circles in half in order to have a base and a lid. On each plate arrange a base, then top with a blanched spinach leaf and poached oysters. Coat with the sauce, then put the puff pastry lid on top. Sprinkle with the cut chervil.

Patrice Caillault

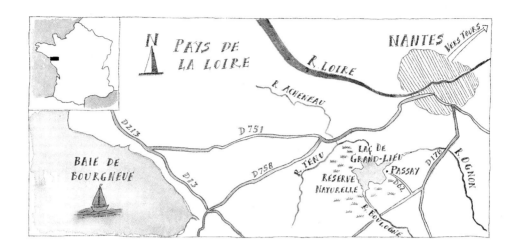

Eels

The village of Passay, not far from Nantes, has a deserted and faintly sinister air about it. Whether this is due to the fact that so many of its inhabitants have moved away in search of employment, or to the enduring effects of an ancient curse, is not easy to determine.

Whatever the case, in a narrow back street of this wan village lives a delightful old couple, almost the last of a traditional group of fisherfolk, Monsieur and Madame Baudray. He is a red-faced man with grey hair and bright eyes tinged with green, and she is an equally lively person of a most hospitable nature.

Passay sits at the edge of the Lac de Grand-Lieu, the largest lake in France, although it varies in size from 6,300 hectares in the winter to 2,600 in the summer (from 15,750 to 6,500 acres) and is nowhere much more than 1.5 m (5 ft) in depth. It has a pleasantly inviolate feeling about it, the lonely stretch of water surrounded by virgin groves of trees. Nothing disturbs the peace, except for the cries of the water birds and the occasional splash of a fish jumping for a fly.

The lake used to belong to Monsieur Guerlain, the head of the family famous as the makers of the best scent in France. A few years ago, the old gentleman, who is now 87, gave the lake to the nation. It was decided to keep it as a nature sanctuary. No tourism is allowed – no water sports, no shooting, no fishing.

M. Guerlain made two conditions when he gave the lake. First, that he should be allowed to come to shoot the duck, which he does nearly every Saturday during the season; secondly, that the fishermen of the village, whose livelihood depended

Eels must be kept alive as long as possible, as they go off quickly. Furthermore, as their blood is poisonous, it is important not to handle them when their skin is broken. To keep them alive, the fisherman has a tank on his boat for his catch.

on the lake, should be allowed to continue to fish as they had always done. There were, not very long ago, 120 fishermen, but now there are only ten, of whom André Baudray is one. Soon there will be none, for the right to fish is not heritable and the few remaining who are entitled to the privilege are not young.

There are many kinds of fish in the lake, but the principal catch is eels. These curious, primeval-seeming creatures, that appear to be the victims of some evolutionary hiccough with their fatiguing life-cycle, are by no means like other fish. There is much dispute and, even today, a fair measure of mystery about this life-cycle. I felt confident that anything M. Baudray told me about eels was bound to be right since he had spent his whole life watching them and earning his living from them, but experts contradict many of the things he believes.

As every schoolboy knows, European freshwater eels spawn in the Sargasso Sea in the Atlantic (to the south-west of Bermuda) and it is there that the young hatch. M. Baudray assured me that it was only the impregnated female that had to make the long journey out to the Sargasso, which struck me as the ultimate in animal male chauvinism, but apparently he is quite mistaken on this point. Both males and females cross the ocean, the males going when they have been in Europe for about six to nine years. The females go from one to three years later when they may be as much as 60 cm (24 in).

The eels, which are sluggish when in fresh water, become active swimmers when in the sea, covering as much as 40–50 km (25–31 miles) a day and reach their breeding ground in three to four months. The precise area is between latitudes 22 and 30 degrees north, centred on 26 degrees north and 56 degrees west. There, at a depth of 100–300 m (330–990 ft), where the water is at a constant 20°C, a colossal nuptial feast takes place.

The young that result *(leptocephali)* are leaf-shaped and transparent. They develop very slowly, taking three years to grow to a length of 7–9 cm (2¾–3¼ in). During that time, both as eggs and as *leptocephali*, they are borne by the Gulf Stream across the Atlantic towards Europe. The crossing is slow, taking about three years. During it, the creatures lose their transparency and become smaller, measuring only 6 cm (2¼ in). They arrive in the first three months of the year, transformed now into elvers. It is a fascinating sight to watch them, in so close a single file that they look like an endless black thread, making their way up a river, hugging the bank for safety. At some point they scatter, the males peeling off earlier than the females. Some make their way overland for considerable distances, until they reach a suitable lake or pond in which to live. Eels can survive out of water for several hours but, as they are vulnerable to predators, they prefer to travel on wet moonless nights.

The eel-fishing season lasts only from March to November, because eels hibernate – at least, M. Baudray says they hibernate, while some experts say they do not, though they do burrow down into the mud to escape cold weather, which seems to me much the same thing. While they are carnivorous and voracious eaters, they can go without food for long periods.

For the first two months of the season, M. Baudray catches his eels with a rod and line. After that the water becomes too warm and so, for reasons that were not clear to me, but partly due to the fact that the area of the lake navigable by boat is reduced to a seventh of what it is in winter, the eels no longer take the bait. Instead, M. Baudray uses nets, which he keeps at a small cabin in the woods by an inlet where his boat is moored. The nets are odd-looking, something like a triple hour-glass, with three compartments. In the lake, across a current, he has constructed a 50 m (55 yd) dam that encourages the eels to swim into the nets.

Baudray's boat is a flat-bottomed craft, not unlike a punt, except that on board he has a small '*vivier*' or tank in which to put his catch, which must be kept alive as eels turn very quickly when dead. Back at his cabin, he transfers them to a larger tank, where they stay until it is time to sell them.

M. Baudray, an independent character, makes his own nets and fishes on his own except for the company of his dog.

He expects his annual catch to be about 30 tons, which is a lot of eels when you realise that a kilo consists of something between nine and thirteen of the wriggling creatures, which means a minimum of 270,000 eels. I thought these figures preposterous until I discovered that each female produces 1.3 to 1.5 million eggs.

Several mysteries remain about eels. The European eel is a widespread species, with no sub-species. They are found in plenty in Italy, Greece and Turkey. If these eastern eels have to go to the Sargasso Sea to breed, they must pass through the Straits of Gibraltar but, according to the Italian expert Paola Manfredi, no-one has ever caught an eel in the Straits. She may have been being too emphatic in saying 'never', but certainly it is virtually unheard of for anyone to see an eel there. But then, there is no record of anyone's seeing an eel on its outward journey in the Atlantic. No-one knows either what becomes of the parent eels after breeding. Do they live on at a great depth, or do they die? As their entire guts regress just before migration to allow space for the rapidly maturing gonads, ovaries and testes, it is unlikely that they survive for long.

Baudray used to deliver his eels all over France, but now the demand has dropped, and he and his wife are inclined to do rather less than they used to. They do, however go on adventurous holidays, having an unexpected admiration for Britain and in particular Scotland, though not for British food.

Madame Baudray is an enthusiastic cook with a liking for the old traditional ways of cooking eels – in a *matelote*, with Malaga grapes, Agen prunes and red wine, stewing them for up to two hours. Baby eels she cooks *à la Provençale* with lots of oil and garlic. Otherwise she grills them with *gros sel* 'as always at the Grand-Lieu'.

It is Madame Baudray who likes to half-believe in the story of the curse, while her husband looks benignly sceptical. 'There was once a village here, called Herbauges, and St Martin came to visit it. He was badly received. It was a bit like the story of Sodom and Gomorrah.' At this point Madame Baudray looked a little shy and asked if I knew that story, but she went on. 'So St Martin cursed the village and it was submerged beneath the lake with its church and all its houses. And at midnight on Christmas Eve, one can hear the bells of the church ringing out from below the water.'

There are not many first-class restaurants that serve eels now. The one supreme exception is Charles Barrier in Tours, in many ways the most distinguished chef in France. He is now 75 and has run his eponymous restaurant for nearly 50 years, gaining three Michelin stars for many of them. The restaurant has been reduced a little in size and M. Barrier now spends fewer hours in the kitchen, but he watches carefully over everything. He is still inventive, but amusingly trenchant in his

The Lac de Grand-Lieu has a wonderfully lonely peace about it. Nothing disturbs the quiet of this almost unique nature reserve.

criticism of anything gimmicky.

He says that not long ago he asked the editors of the *Guide Michelin* whether he should go on producing old-fashioned dishes like stuffed pig's trotters and his glorious *matelote d'anguilles*, for which he gave us the recipe. The response was: 'Please, M. Barrier, never stop because, if you do not do these things, surely, nobody else will.'

There is a sad comparison to be made between these two charming and elderly gentlemen. They are the last of their kind. M. Baudray is one of the last fishermen on the Lac de Grand-Lieu. And Charles Barrier, who was a chef of distinction long before Paul Bocuse and his *bande* were ever heard of, represents an age and a style that he has kept alive for so long and that will disappear completely when he finally retires. We will miss them.

Terrine de poisson

FISH TERRINE

Makes 2 terrines
2 pieces of eel, about 800 g (1¾ lb)
1 salmon, about 1.5 kg (3¼ lb) in weight
250 g (9 oz) monkfish
2 litres (3½ pints) fish stock
fine rashers of streaky bacon or barding fat to
line and cover the terrines
2 large lemons, sliced very thinly
1 kg (2¼ lb) mushrooms, trimmed and sautéed
in butter
50 g (2 oz) shallots, peeled and finely chopped
2 tablespoons freshly chopped parsley
50 g (2 oz) anchovy fillets, finely chopped
Panada
125g (4½ oz) butter
400 ml (14 fl oz) milk
190 g (6½ oz) plain flour
6 egg yolks
Terrine filling
1.5 kg (3¼ lb) pike flesh
250 g (9 oz) butter
8 egg whites
120 ml (4 fl oz) jellied fish stock
120 ml (4 fl oz) Cognac
cayenne pepper and freshly grated nutmeg
salt and pepper
250 g (9 oz) shelled pistachio nuts, chopped
125 g (4½ oz) truffles, chopped

Clean the eel, salmon and monkfish, and fillet them, removing all bones and skins. Cook very lightly in the fish stock, simmering for only a few minutes. Drain and allow to cool. Reserve the fish stock.

Preheat the oven to its lowest setting.

For the panada, very gently melt the butter in the milk. Add the flour, salt, pepper, cayenne and nutmeg, and beat well until the mixture leaves the sides of the pan. Add the egg yolks one at a time, beating in well.

Place panada in a blender and add most of the terrine filling ingredients – the pike, butter, egg whites, jellied stock and Cognac. Season. Blend, then stir in the nuts and truffles.

Line the terrine dishes with most of the bacon or barding fat, then with the lemon slices. Fill with layers of stuffing, fish fillets, mushrooms and a mixture of the shallots, parsley and anchovy. Top with the remaining bacon or barding fat.

Place the terrine dishes in a bain-marie and cook in the very low oven for about 3 hours. At the end of the cooking time, put a little of the reserved fish stock into the dishes around the sides. Do not over-fill. Leave to become cold. Serve with a Sauce Vincent, made with equal quantities of blanched and chopped herbs (watercress, tarragon, parsley, chervil, chives and spinach), folded into a mixture of two-thirds *crème fraîche* and one-third mayonnaise.

Matelote d'anguilles au Bourgueil

EEL STEWED IN RED WINE

For 6

3 medium eels, about 2 kg (4½ lb) total weight
200 g (7 oz) butter
2 tablespoons *marc* (brandy distilled from the
pips, skins etc of wine-making)
1 garlic clove, peeled and chopped
200 g (7 oz) large onions, peeled and chopped
1 *bouquet garni* (bay leaves, parsley, 1 small
onion, pierced with cloves)
100 ml (3½ fl oz) *crème fraîche*
salt and pepper
Garnish
12 prunes
1 litre (1¾ pints) Bourgueil wine (a red wine
from Touraine)
12 small onions, peeled
100 g (4 oz) butter
a pinch of sugar
150 g (5 oz) *lardons* (see page 123)
100 g (4 oz) white mushrooms, cleaned
8 pieces of toast, shaped like hearts

The garnish: Soak the prunes in the wine for 24 hours. Drain, retaining the wine, and stone the prunes. Put both aside until needed.

Preheat the oven to 180°C(350°F) Gas 4.

In a small casserole, sauté the small onions in a quarter of the butter with the sugar and some salt. Cover with water and cook in the preheated oven until light brown, about 30 minutes. Drain, and keep warm with the prunes, in the oven reduced to warm.

Put the *lardons* into a saucepan of cold water and bring to the boil. Refresh in cold water, then drain and fry them in a third of the remaining butter. Drain, and add to the prunes and onions.

Fry the mushrooms lightly in the same pan as the *lardons*, adding a little butter. Drain. Fry the heart-shaped *croûtons* in the remaining butter until golden. Drain and keep the mushrooms and *croûtons* warm with the other garnish ingredients.

The eels: Ask the fishmonger to clean and skin the eels. Cut them into 10 cm (4 in) pieces. Soak for 15 minutes in cold water.

Put the wine used for the prunes into a saucepan and boil to reduce by half.

Drain and dry the fish pieces. In a suitable casserole, fry them in half the butter until brown. Add the *marc* and *flambé*. Pour the reduced wine over the eels together with the garlic, the chopped onions and the *bouquet garni*. Poach the eel as slowly as possible on a very low heat for 15 minutes. It is cooked when the pieces feel tender to the touch. Drain them and put aside in the warm oven.

To serve: Boil to reduce the remaining liquid by half, then strain. Add the warm garnish ingredients, apart from the *croûtons*, and let simmer for 5 minutes. Add the remaining butter in pieces and the *crème fraîche*. Stir over a very low heat, and season to taste.

Pour the reduced liquid over the pieces of eel and simmer for 1-2 minutes. Garnish with the *croûtons* and serve hot.

Charles Barrier

Mushrooms

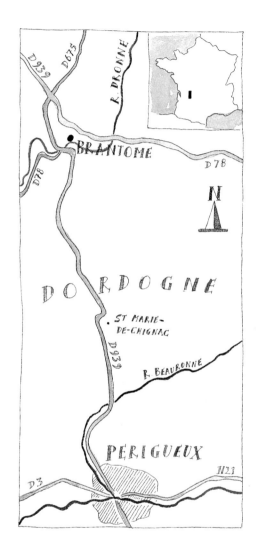

Mushrooms have about them an aura of mystery. They belong, somehow, in the realms of fairies and sorcery. They are strangely potent, capable of inducing wild hallucinations – even, if we are to believe some sources, the mainspring of mystical religion. And they can be deadly. Admittedly, out of the 3,000 or more kinds of mushrooms found in Europe not many are fatal, but those that are have cruel characteristics. They may sometimes lurk in the body for nearly three weeks before giving any hint that they are working away, destroying the liver or the kidneys, by which time it is too late to do anything about it.

The names we give them, whether in English or in French, have a curious ring – Trooping Crumble Cap, Destroying Angel, Herald of Winter, Lawyer's Wig, Judas Ear, Monk's Head, Horn of Plenty. This last the French call *Trompette de la mort*, not because it is poisonous, for in fact it is delicious, but because its black shape conjured up for them the image of the Moorish invaders' trumpets and thus death.

Unlike all other plants, if they can be called plants, mushrooms live a nefarious kind of life, not creating their sustenance by photosynthesis, but by stealing their nourishment from other vegetable matter by way of their *mycelium*, the gossamer network that constitutes their main existence, often as fine as a spider's thread, broadly spread, but hidden invisible below the surface of the earth.

The French are eager gatherers and eaters of mushrooms, secretly hoarding the knowledge of where this or that variety of fungus may grow, never seemingly put off by the repulsive appearance of so many of the most succulent species. The one held in the highest esteem is the *cèpe (Boletus edulis)*, known in English as the cep or Penny Bun, which grows most readily in oak and beech woods. The forests of

In Périgord, the mushroom season brings out hundreds of enthusiastic searchers hoping to find wild mushrooms, especially the cèpe.

Périgord are as famous for their *cèpes* as they are for their truffles.

We went to Brantôme, a town with an atmosphere that matches in some ways the primeval nature of mushrooms. The river Dronne, winding this way and that, has formed over the millennia steep cliffs, honeycombed with caves and natural grottoes. In these, prehistoric man lived and men ever since have adapted them to their needs, so that even today there are people living in troglodyte style, the opening to their caves being filled with the wall and windows of an ordinary house.

In the time of Charlemagne, between the cliff and the river, monks of the order of Saint Benoît built an abbey, opposite an island formed by a fork in the river, which is now the site of the town. Of the 70 or so abbots who governed the abbey until the last Benedictine monks left at the time of the Revolution, the most famous was Pierre de Bourdeille, commonly known simply as Brantôme. This far from devout person, who was never ordained and never took any vows, least of all of chastity, so intrigues historians that eight books have been written about him since the Second World War in English alone.

In 1557, Henri II made him the Abbot of Brantôme at the age of seventeen. He accompanied Mary, Queen of Scots to Scotland when she assumed her throne, and managed on the same journey to visit Queen Elizabeth. The rest of his life he spent fighting in Africa for the Portuguese, for the Knights of Malta against the Sultan, and in France against the Protestants. When he was not fighting he was making love. Nonetheless, we owe the preservation of the town of Brantôme to his tolerance. Because of his refusal to persecute Protestants, whenever during the religious wars they had a chance to destroy the town, they spared it.

The Abbot's fame today is due to his prolific writings, in fifteen solid volumes, about life at court in the seventeenth century and especially to his *Dames Galantes*, a lively account of his endless amorous adventures with fashionable ladies.

The old mill of the abbey is now a hotel with an excellent restaurant where Christian Ravinel cooks for half the year, the tourist season in Périgord being short. In the winter, he goes to Courchevel where the owner has another hotel. He is most insistent, wherever he is, on using the local produce, so that mushrooms feature prominently on his menu. He invited his principal supplier and his wife to lunch with us at the Moulin de l'Abbaye.

René Naboulet was a nervous and shy countryman, whose eyebrows shot up and down whenever anyone spoke to him. He and his wife looked so alike that they might have been brother and sister. They both had hazel eyes and extraordinarily long ear-lobes, and they wore their grizzled hair cut short. Their absurdly rosy cheeks puffed up in identical smiles. When I asked whether they came from the same region, they said by no means; they were born at least twenty miles from each other.

The Naboulets led us to their farm, half an hour out of Brantôme on the way to Perigueux. It was a small house, lost in rolling country, surrounded by a little land that they work as a market garden, and 17.5 hectares (43¾ acres) of woodland. They are practically self-sufficient, growing nearly everything they eat, making their own wine and even a fortified drink a little like *Floc de Gascogne* (see page 43). By the front door, perched out of reach of the animals, were two of the biggest loaves of bread I have ever seen, one of the few things they do not make themselves. When they saw us gazing in surprise, they said, 'You see we are simple people, we eat a lot of bread.'

Of all the things that grow on his land, it is the mushrooms that excite René Naboulet the most. One gets the feeling that he considers the understanding of the quixotic ways of fungi a greater skill than the planting and harvesting of ordinary plants. René inherited the land from his father, but it is a point of pride with him that he found his own locations where the various mushrooms spring up. In March it is the *morels (Morchella esculenta)*, in April the *mousserons (Marasmius oreades* or Fairy Ring *champignons)* and in late May the first of the *cèpes*, 'that is if the moon is

The exact locations where cèpes grow are assiduously guarded. M. Naboulet, walking through his woods, covers his tracks, rearranging the leaves with his talisman stick from Lourdes.

not late as it was this year, so that they did not come till early June.'

It is, of course, a matter of first importance that no-one else should ever discover where these secret places are. Each day as he goes out, René carries with him a cane that he bought in Lourdes for good fortune and for protection from all ills. For instance, many wild boar frequent his woods and they are dangerous. The cane serves, too, to cover his tracks. With it he gently arranges the leaves so that no-one can tell where he has been.

Nothing about mushrooms is totally predictable. Everyone knows, for example, that after a good spell of rain the *cèpes* will be plentiful. Cars queue up in the lanes around Brantôme, but their drivers, foraging in the woods, go away empty-handed. It is probably the fault of the moon.

It is in many ways a matter of instinct to know when the mushrooms will spring up and timing is significant because a *cèpe* can grow to its full size in two days and it is too old to be worth picking in a week.

There are other, more lasting, mysteries. In the 1940s, during much of which decade René was, for reasons which he says he never understood, a prisoner of war in Germany, the heads of the *cèpes* grew so large that they did not bother to keep the stalks. Mushrooms, like every other wild product that we looked at, have apparently suffered from agricultural pollution, though it is hard to say exactly in what way, as sometimes they seem to thrive on land that has been sprayed and sometimes disappear altogether.

There is no question today of throwing away the stalks, for in the market at Perigueux, where the Naboulets have a stall every Saturday, *cèpes* sell for £7 or £8 a kg (2¼ lb).

The first thing René does when he comes back from the woods with his basket lined with bracken is to weigh what he has picked. All suppliers of produce taken from nature are reluctant to reveal how much they manage to pick or glean or catch, because they have a terror of the taxman reading about their true earnings. René Naboulet says that he gathers only 200 kg (440 lb) a year, which, even at £8 a kg, hardly represents much of a living. His enthusiasm reflects more a labour of love.

Christian Ravinel, who claims that the whole region smells of mushrooms, loves working with them and his salad incorporating *cèpes* with goat's cheese is memorable. His other recipe uses the other regional speciality – duck.

Charlotte de canard confit aux cèpes

CHARLOTTE OF PRESERVED DUCK WITH
CEPES

For 4
500 g (18 oz) *cèpes*
4 legs of preserved duck (*confit*)
4 large green cabbage leaves
50g (2 oz) butter
1 bunch of flat parsley, washed and coarsely
chopped
150 ml (5 fl oz) *crème fraîche*
salt and pepper

Boil the cabbage leaves in salted water until
tender. Drain, refresh in cold water, then
drain again and cool. Using a little of the
butter, grease four small ovenproof dishes,
10 cm (4 in) in diameter, and arrange a cabbage leaf inside each one as a lining.

Preheat the oven to 200°C(400°F) Gas 6.

Bone the duck legs and half fill each dish
with the meat. Keep in a cool place.

Wipe the mushroom heads, and peel and
wash the stalks. Mince the heads and the
stalks separately. Fry the heads and stalks
separately in the remaining butter, then season. Divide the chopped parsley between the
two.

Heat the cream, add the minced stalks and
parsley to it, then put in the blender to make
a smooth sauce.

Fill the ramekins with the minced *cèpe*
head mixture, cover with foil, and bake in a
bain-marie in the preheated oven for 15
minutes. Remove from the ramekins and
serve hot with the sauce.

A *confit* consists of pieces of duck (or
goose) salted, cooked and preserved in
their own fat. *Confits* can be made at
home, but can also be found in good
food stores.

Rocamadour rôti aux cèpes

CABECOUS DE ROCAMADOUR ROASTED
WITH CEPES

For 4
400 g (14 oz) *cèpes*
4 *cabécous* (small goat cheeses)
100 g 4(oz) pork caul fat (*crépine*), soaked in
cold water
20 g (¾ oz) unsalted butter
1 bunch of flat parsley, washed and chopped
To serve
4 kinds of lettuce (radicchio, batavia, frisée,
oakleaf), washed and dried
4 tablespoons walnut oil
1 tablespoon old wine vinegar

Wash, drain and dry the caul fat, then cut
into four equal pieces.

Peel and wash the stalks of the *cèpes*, then
dry. Wipe the heads of the *cèpes*. Cut the
stalks into tiny dice then fry in half the butter
until soft. Keep warm. Cut the *cèpe* heads
into tiny dice and fry in the remaining butter
until soft. Add the parsley.

Coat each cheese with the *cèpe* head and
parsley mixture, and wrap in a quarter of the
caul fat. Put under a very hot grill for 3-4
minutes. Serve hot with a nut bread and the
salad leaves dressed with walnut oil and
vinegar, and the fried *cèpe* stalks.

Christian Ravinel

Cabécous, also known as *cabécous de
Rocamadour*, are tiny discs of cheese, made
with sheep's milk in the spring and goat's
milk in the summer. Slices of any circular
goat's cheese may be substituted.

Caul fat or *crépine* is the thin membrane
from the stomach lining of the pig, which
contains veins of fat. It is used in home-
made sausages, faggots and *crépinettes*. It
can be ordered from good butchers.

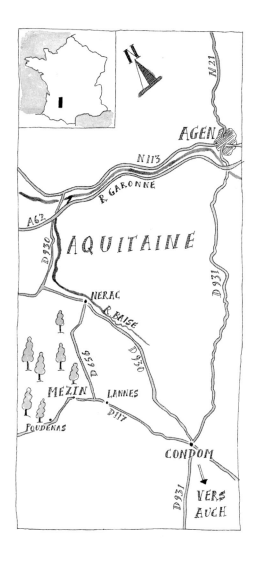

Foie Gras

Poudenas is one of those miraculously undisturbed villages in that region of south-western France that has, in its time, been part of Aquitaine, Gascony, Navarre or whatever, and happens now to be in the department of Lot-et-Garonne. A fine seventeenth-century castle, set in a luxurious wood, dominates the village which tumbles steeply down the hillside below the castle walls.

At the bottom runs a river that marks the edge of the village. There is a romantic, half-timbered, old building called the Hôtel du Roi and near it is a medieval house with the scallop shell of St Jacques over the door, showing this to have been a stopping place for pilgrims on their way to Santiago de Compostela. A little further along beside the river is an old mill, by a bridge, now the Auberge de la Belle Gasconne. It is all far prettier than a picture.

La Belle Gasconne, one must take it, is Madame Gracia who with her husband runs the Auberge. More importantly, it is she who cooks the rich food of the region in their restaurant, on the opposite side of the road from the mill inn. Madame Gracia is a native of Poudenas. Indeed, her father owned the Hôtel du Roi, which is now little more than a rather grumpy bar, and one might wonder why she did not run that. Even in so idyllic a place as Poudenas, there are tensions of which one does not speak. Suffice it to say that her staff eat their daily meals in one corner of the old building and that is that.

Furthermore, it may never have been her original intention to run a restaurant. When they married, she and her husband became farmers whose principal business was raising geese for *foie gras*.

There can be no other food that provokes the furious passions that *foie gras* arouses, nor one so bedevilled by myth. The morally squeamish eagerly embrace tales of birds, with their feet nailed to the floor beside the farmhouse hearth, being brutally force-fed for weeks on end and undergoing untold suffering in the name of gastronomy.

The facts are very different. M. Gracia was indignant at the suggestion that there was any cruelty involved in the production of *foie gras*, advancing, at first, the justification that the Romans had eaten *foie gras* and that he had seen at Merouk, in Egypt, carvings showing that the ancient Egyptians used exactly the same techniques as those used today in Europe. (I have never found this a very convincing argument because, it seems to me, one could, on the grounds of antique custom, make a good case in favour of cannibalism.) But a few minutes with Madame Gracia would convince anyone that this warm-hearted and generous woman could never have a part in anything brutal.

The Gracias emphasised the importance of the relationship between the producer and his birds. 'Every producer pretends that he has some special secret. One says he feeds the birds once a day, another says twice, yet another three times. Someone else will say that he uses red maize or white maize, but truly there is nothing in all of that. The one thing that is important is that the geese or the ducks are well cared for. They must love the person that feeds them.'

They pointed out that the birds live a perfectly free life out of doors until they reach the age when their wings cross over each other at the back, which is to say at about four months. The *gavage*, or forced feeding – at any rate for ducks – lasts for a matter of only twelve days. 'The object is not to produce an enormous bird, but to develop its liver well. It is best to start with a fat duck, but a huge liver is not good.'

A recent scandal about the treatment of ducks by the large industrial producers of *foie gras de canard* resulted in Switzerland's banning all imports of *foie gras*. They were accused of cutting off the ends of the creatures' beaks to make it easier to force-feed them. Although ducks, the Gracias agreed, were more difficult to feed, especially Barbary ducks (a variety descended from Muscovy ducks), they maintained that it was unthinkable that any Gascon farmer would think of doing such a thing. If they had a particularly awkward duck, they used to let it go.

French *foie gras* has not been having an easy time lately. In 1990, national production reached a record total of 6,000 tons. The following year it was down to 4,000 tons. This was largely due to the importation of cheap *foie gras* from Hungary, other Eastern European countries and even Israel. The inevitable result of this has been a reluctance on the part of banks to help producers and a consequent drop in quality.

None of this affects Madame Gracia, in whose restaurant one gets nothing but the highest quality, both of produce and of cooking. She, as a former producer, knows what she wants. Nonetheless she buys only separate livers, because one

Left: *M.Cescalti loves his ducks. The relationship between breeder and duck or goose is a very close one. If not, it is impossible to persuade the bird to accept gavage.* Right: *The life of the* foie gras *geese is by no means unpleasant.*

cannot judge the exact quality and condition from the outside of a bird.

Madame Gracia's main supplier, Alain Cescalti, lives on a farm not 5 km (3 miles) away, just outside the small town of Mézin. He bore out, both in manner and in what he said, everything that the Gracias had told us.

Alain is a handsome, bearded man of 33, his dark brown eyes revealing his Italian origins. He has nothing of the look of a traditional French peasant, going bareheaded and preferring bright shorts and a T-shirt. He is a gentle person, devoted to his young wife and their two children. It would be difficult to imagine his indulging in any barbarity.

Alain has 20 hectares (50 acres) of land on which he keeps 1,800 ducks and 200 geese. The geese are a cross between the *Oie de Toulouse* and the *Oie des Landes*, the latter being smaller. The ducks are also a cross, being half Peking and half Barbary, a mixture that produces a bird known as *mulard*, which is, like a mule, incapable of reproduction. It has the advantage of a meat that tastes good as well as a fine liver.

Alain does not breed his birds. To both breed and produce raises too many problems of hygiene. He buys day-old chicks, keeps them indoors for a fortnight and then turns them out for their four months in the open. The ducks live in the pastures bordering a lake. The only thing that appeared in any way unkind was that the lake was fenced off so that they could not go to it. The reason is that new chicks arrive every four weeks and each group must be kept separate; moreover, the pastures have to be rotated regularly to avoid disease, so the lake is out of bounds. Each group of 200 ducks needs living space of nearly a hectare (2½ acres).

The geese, which eat a lot of grass, were living in a larger area, a long sloping field, with views across the valley leading to Poudenas. Foxes are for them a major hazard. Alain has installed lights to deter them, 'but nothing puts them off, they still come. They jump fences, they dig under them, they even manage somehow to cut them.' The sad evidence of a fox's raid lay in the field as we went through it. But there was at the same time happier evidence of the geese's trust in Alain. They crowded round him with no expectation of food.

'To do this job you must like it and like the creatures. I started when I was fifteen. My mother had an accident and I had to take over. It is essential that only one person performs the *gavage*. One cannot change over in the middle; the handler who starts must finish. Geese are very sensitive about this, so one must try never to be ill.'

The *gavage* is not the horrible thing that it is made out to be. It takes place in a special building that is kept always at a temperature of 10°C. Nowadays it is done mechanically. Alain puts a tube down the bird's throat and a pump drives the maize down. The process lasts 30 seconds. He feeds the ducks twice a day for ten to twelve days, giving them a kilogram (2¼ lb) of maize at each feed. The geese are fed three times a day, equally with a kilogram, and their *gavage* lasts 17 to 25 days.

'The birds are a little unhappy for the first couple of days, but I think that is due more to the change from their outdoor life than to any discomfort. After that, they settle down and accept their feeding without any trouble.'

I left Alain's farm well satisfied that, for all the fuss, there are many far more brutal things done to animals by food manufacturers than ever befell a Gascon goose.

Of course, in these days of food faddism, another charge laid against *foie gras* is that it must be unhealthy, fat being anathema to diet freaks. Recent research provides much merriment in this realm. The people of south-western France eat twice as much *foie gras* as other Frenchmen and at least 50 times as much as, say, the average American. In America, every year, 315 out of 100,000 middle-aged men die of heart attacks. In France generally, the figure is 145. In Toulouse, not far from the heart of *foie gras* country, the comparable number is only 80.

These statistics are deeply paining to American scientists, who are driven to wonder, contrary to all accepted health lore, whether France's better health is not due to a mixture of wine, olive oil and *foie gras* – three delights of gastronomy.

Salade de l'auberge

SALAD OF DUCK *FOIE GRAS*

For 4
150 g (5 oz) cooked duck *foie gras*
250 g (9 oz) French beans, topped and tailed
100 g (4 oz) watermelon flesh, seeded carefully
1 large pear, peeled
1 small lettuce, washed and dried
2 large mushrooms, trimmed and sliced
a few mint leaves
salt and pepper
Tomato coulis
2 tomatoes, skinned and seeded
juice of 1 lemon
4-5 fresh mint leaves
1½ tablespoons olive oil
Tarragon coulis
8 tarragon sprigs, very finely chopped
100 ml (3½ fl oz) *crème fraîche*
juice of 1 lemon
Vinaigrette
1 tablespoon sherry vinegar
2 tablespoons grapeseed oil

Begin by cooking the French beans. Boil them in salted water, uncovered, for only 8 minutes. Drain and cool under cold water.

For the tomato *coulis*, put all the ingredients into a blender and purée. Season and keep cool.

For the tarragon *coulis*, mix the tarragon leaves with the cream and lemon juice. Season with salt and pepper and keep cool.

For the vinaigrette, beat the vinegar and oil with some salt and pepper, and reserve.

To prepare the salad, slice the watermelon flesh into very thin strips, like transparent slices of Parma ham. Cut the pear into very thin slices lengthwise, cutting off any core.

Arrange the dried lettuce leaves equally on each plate. Place the French beans, the slices of pear, watermelon and mushroom equally on each plate. Season with the vinaigrette.

Slice the cooked *foie gras* thinly and lay some on each salad. With a small brush, put a coat of vinaigrette on each slice to make them glossy. Garnish with the mint leaves and serve with the two *coulis*.

Tartine de foie gras au Floc de Gascogne

HOT *FOIE GRAS* TOAST

'This recipe has to be tasted by two people in love, with a little hunger but a lot of greed!'

Per tartine (toast)
1 centre slice of a large round crusty loaf
2 slices, 2 cm (¾ in) thick, of fresh duck *foie gras*
slices of fresh seasonal fruit (see below) to cover the *tartine*
4 tablespoons *Floc de Gascogne* (or very good port)
1 dessertspoon fruit vinegar
2 glasses of above chosen alcohol

Brown the *foie gras* slices briefly in a frying pan on each side as for calves' liver. Pour the fat into another pan, and fry briefly in it, according to season, slices of fresh fruits (peaches, pears, figs, etc).

Toast the slice of bread until golden brown but still soft. When the *foie gras* is cooked, still pink, place it on the warm bread. Keep warm.

Boil the alcohol and vinegar together to reduce by three-quarters in the frying pan in which you cooked the *foie gras*. When ready, pour over the slices of fruits in the other pan. The fruits become red and lacquered in the boiling sauce. Place on top of the *foie gras*.

With one person at each end, start biting into the toast and devouring each other with the eyes. Have a break from time to time and sip your glass of *Floc* or port. When your lips join, it's time to say 'I love you'.

Mme Gracia

Floc de Gascogne is a mixture of fresh grape juice and Armagnac. It is sometimes available in good stores in Britain. (A similar drink from further north is *Pineau de Charente*, a mixture of fresh grape juice and Cognac.)

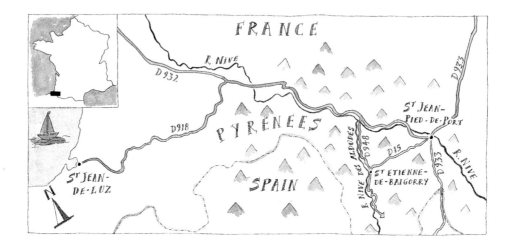

Brebis Cheese

The valley of Baïgorry (also spelled Baïgorrie or Baïgorri) lies on the French slopes of the Pyrenees, not far inland from the Atlantic. It is not really wild country, nor even very harsh. While the valley is steep and mountainous and one might expect its climate to be severe, it is in fact quite mild. In winter it never gets very cold – perhaps a couple of dozen frosts a year and four or five falls of snow – and in the summer it is cool.

At the same time, there is a strangeness, a pervading sense of unfamiliarity about the place. At first, it is hard to decide what to attribute this foreign quality to. The landscape is pretty enough, noticeably unspoilt in fact. The lower, dome-shaped hills, their green smoothness patterned with stone walls rather like a hairnet, are unusual, but not odd. The architecture is different: the houses are mostly plain white with red-tiled roofs, their doors and windows having surrounds of red sandstone, reminding one of houses in Celtic countries.

In the end, I decided that it was a feeling that this land was somehow ancient and everlasting and set apart. Man has plainly lived here for many centuries, even many thousands of years, and there are, among the hills, dolmens and cromlechs to prove the early occupation of the region. There are Roman bridges, old Navarre castles, the remains of fortifications dating from the Peninsular War, and traces of the Spanish Civil War, the Spanish border being only a few short miles away – a whole chaotic history.

The farmhouses of this gentle valley in the Pyrenees are simple, and have mostly remained in the same families for many generations, the owners often being known by the name of the original builders of the house.

But there is more to it than that, for this is Basque country, part of the old kingdom of Navarre, and lived in by a people whose origins no-one knows, people of an enduringly rebellious and independent nature.

Beside the River Nive at St-Etienne-de-Baïgorry is a hotel and restaurant called simply Arcé. This is a well-known name in the valley. There was a champion of the Basque version of the game, pelota (played here with bare hands) called Amédée Arcé, an uncle of Pascal Arcé.

Pascal, a handsome, brown-eyed young man with black curly hair, is the fifth generation of his family to run the inn. His 91-year-old grandmother still wanders around looking helpful. The restaurant has had a Michelin star for years and Pascal is a chef of high quality. He has worked in London, Paris, Bordeaux, and San Francisco, but he sticks, for the most part, to very traditional dishes. Many of his recipes are his father's and may be 20 to 30 years old. He sees no reason to change something that he considers to be good. As with all chefs, he likes cooking fish more than anything else. Here he has the advantage of the river and, below the outside games room, there is a place to keep the trout alive in the river water.

There is one unexpected dish that is entirely regional. It is the *caillé* or *mamilla*, the fresh curds of sheep's milk – a sort of junket. Here, ewe's milk is also made into a remarkable cheese which Pascal serves with raisin bread, walnuts and quince jam. When we talked about this, Pascal said he wanted us to meet his supplier of sheep's cheese, whom he called 'the poet'.

It took some time to establish what the cheese-maker's name was, for local farmers have two if not three names: first is their name in French, then the Basque version of it and often, owing to the old laws of inheritance in the region, the name of the family that originally built and owned the house they live in. A house could be inherited by a man or a woman who would keep the name going. The heir or heiress presumptive always married a junior member of another family, so that there was no danger of a farm passing into that other family. If for reasons of poverty the house was sold, other members of the family had an automatic right to buy it back at the same price. It was not until the late seventeenth century that people took their father's surnames.

Raymond Marticorena, a strongly-made man in his early thirties, is also known as Eramoun Marticorena. His house is a fine example of the solid farmhouses built at the beginning of the nineteenth century, with a grand lintel over the main doorway, with a motto and the date, 1834. Inside, it is simple, with earthen floors and a sparse amount of furniture.

Here he lives with his mother who, unexpectedly, was born in the United States. There was, in the last century and the first half of this one, a massive exodus of Basques from this area, first to South America and later to the USA. While many succeeded (Senator Paul Laxalt, President Reagan's special adviser, was the son of a woman from Baïgorry), others were less happy, determinedly preserving their traditions and culture, acquiring curiously little from their adopted country. Many came back and picked up the old threads, preferring their discomforts and hardships to the ways of the new world.

Raymond's life is really little different from that of his ancestors over the centuries. There is nothing transatlantic about his mother or himself. He tends his flock of 100 *manex* (or, in French, *manèche tête roux*) ewes, harvests some hay and makes his cheese.

He is one of the last individual producers of sheep's cheese. The majority of farmers now sell their milk to a co-operative which makes cheese industrially. 'You can tell the industrial cheeses easily, because they are very dry and they have holes in them. A proper cheese should be smooth, with a little taste of salt and acid on the tip of the tongue and a rich taste further back.' Much of the quality is lost in pasteurisation which is obligatory for industrial makers.

Cheese-making is a very precise business. Raymond heats the milk to exactly 33°C when it turns to *caillé*. The *caillé* is left for half an hour. When it separates into curds and whey, he leaves the curds to sink and then presses them by hand into a mould. The pressing at this stage lasts about three hours. He then leaves the *pâte*, as he calls it, for twelve hours before salting it.

Over the doorways of the old houses, there are often mottoes and the date when they were built. At home M. Marticorena is an industrious cheese-maker; out on the hillsides with his sheep, he is a free poetical spirit.

Then he reheats the *pâte* to 38°C and, when it thickens so that it sticks to the palm of the hand held upside-down, it is ready for the pressing machine. For the first hour he applies 1 kg (2¼ lb) of pressure, for the next hour 2 kg (4½ lb), then for another two hours 2.5 kg (5½ lb). It is not difficult this whole process, but it is slow and must be precise, and is nowadays further complicated by interfering directives from the busybodies of the EC, involving expensive new equipment and machinery. For the whole winter, while the sheep are in, Raymond performs each timed step with meticulous care, producing every year a ton and a half of delicious cheese. In January and February, as well as making his cheese, he is also occupied with the lambing.

When the summer comes, his life changes completely, forsaking all that is modern and embracing the familiar. He becomes even more Basque; Raymond becomes Eramoun, as it were. The sheep go up on to the high communal pastures,

The new regulations of the EC have meant that this traditional cheese-maker has had to refurbish all the manufacturing part of his farm in order to obey the fussy dictates of people who are threatening to take the good taste out of traditional food.

and Eramoun wanders with them, paying no attention to the Spanish border, but behaving as if this were still the kingdom of Navarre as indeed, emotionally, it is.

Unlike other regions, such as nearby Béarn, where the *transhumance*, as the summer migration is called, takes place, the people of the Baïgorry Valley make no cheese when the flocks are out. Sometimes, when he is cutting the hay down below at the farm, Eramoun will let the sheep roam by themselves for as long as three days at a stretch, but much of the time he will spend with them in happy freedom, for he is in many ways a solitary man.

It is in the no-man's-land of these lost, high pastures that Eramoun can earn his reputation as a poet. He never had much formal education, having left school at fourteen, but he is steeped in the lore of Basque culture – so much of it passed on by story-tellers and in song – and he speaks three languages. So, as he pastures his sheep, Eramoun sings, at first traditional songs in Basque and French then, after practising them, he goes on to compose his own songs, his rather gentle voice sailing across the steep, green valleys.

Summer, too, is the time for festivals and fairs. The 'poet' is invited to them all and asked to sing. His songs have become so popular in the region that he has cut two records and made a tape.

When the land turns red with the colour of autumn, richer here for no logical reason, and at last fades to the drab of winter, the sheep come in. Raymond, re-stored, goes back to his vats and his presses, and a time that is measured in exact minutes instead of in carefree, loosely bound days.

Le pot de caillé de Brebis ou mamilla

EWE'S MILK JUNKET

For 6
1 litre (1¾ pints) fresh ewe's milk
1 sugar lump
3 ml (a scant teaspoon) rennet

You will need a thermometer graded from 20-100°C(68-212°F).

Heat the milk with the sugar to a temperature of 80°C(176°F). Keep stirring so that the milk doesn't stick to the pan. Sieve the milk through a fine sieve into a dish and let it begin to cool.

When the temperature has reduced to 50°C(122°F), add the rennet and stir in well. Pour into six ovenproof terracotta dishes, 10 cm (4 in) high and 6 cm (2½ in) in diameter.

Let the milk set for 2 hours without moving the dishes, then chill in the fridge. Cover the dishes with foil.

Mamilla is the name for *caillé* in Basque.

L'assiette de fromage de Brebis au membrillo

SHEEP'S CHEESE WITH QUINCE PASTE

Per person

Take a Brebis sheep's cheese which has been kept at a temperature of 23°C(73°F), and cut two thin slices from it. Place on a plate with some quince paste or jam, decorate with walnuts and serve with raisin bread.

Pâte de coings or *cotignac* is the French name for a thick paste or cheese made from puréed quinces. It is known as *membrillo* in Spain.

Les ris d'agneau sautés aux échalottes

LAMB SWEETBREADS SAUTÉED WITH SHALLOTS

Per person
250 g (9 oz) lamb's sweetbreads, trimmed and soaked in cold water overnight
a little white wine vinegar
½ tablespoon olive oil
3 shallots, peeled and chopped
2 *cèpes,* cleaned and sliced
5 white mushrooms, wiped and sliced
15 g (½ oz) butter
1 small garlic clove, peeled and sliced
½ tablespoon fresh chopped parsley
salt and paprika
a cooked puff pastry shape to garnish

Place the sweetbreads in fresh cold salted water with the vinegar, and bring just up to simmering point. Drain.

Meanwhile heat the oil in a frying pan and sauté the shallots, *cèpes* and mushrooms for a few minutes until starting to change colour. Add the sweetbreads and sauté until brown, about 5 minutes.

Pour the oil from the pan, and add the butter, some salt and a little paprika. Add the garlic and parsley, and cook for 30 seconds.

Serve on a plate with the puff pastry garnish (a small crescent, for example).

Pascal Arcé

49

Armagnac

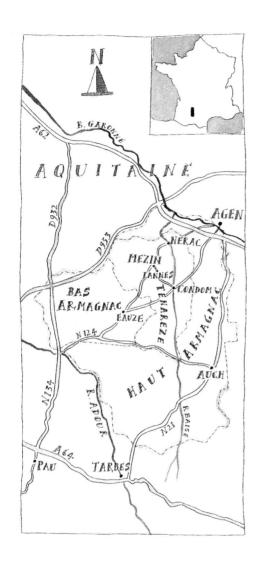

Gascony is so wonderfully sleepy, the hills rolling easily as if they wanted to make no great demands on anyone. The ancient castles, robbed by the centuries of any menace, fit neatly into the somnolent landscape as if tucked up for the night. The castle owners – for instance, the Dukes of Montesquieu in theirs for 850 years, the de Gallards in theirs for 1,050 – give one to think that nothing ever changes here. Yet the history of the region is one of turbulence and strife. What now seems lost was from earliest times a busy and productive area. The main Roman roads to Bordeaux and to northern Spain passed through Gascony as, later, did the pilgrim route to Santiago de Compostela. The religious wars of France were fought over the territory.

The word Gascon derives from Vascon, itself a variation of Basque. Their particular branch was overlaid by the Visigoths, which may account for the fiery temperament we associate with d'Artagnan. Whatever the case, it was the Gascons who developed the first brandy to be drunk for pure pleasure in France. In the Middle Ages, the apothecaries made *aqua ardente* to revive the dying and as a prophylactic in times of plague and other sinister epidemics. It was about the time of the Reformation that the farmers of Gascony transformed this rough spirit into Armagnac. By the middle of the nineteenth century, production of the brandy had reached a peak of some 100,000 hectolitres (about 2½ million gallons).

Cognac started later than Armagnac, but had the advantage of being nearer the sea and the possibility of export, so that today for every litre of Armagnac that is

The tranquil landscapes of present-day Gascony belie its turbulent past.

sold Cognac sells ten. For my taste, Armagnac has a more interesting character because its method of production, with only one distillation as opposed to Cognac's two, leaves it with a more natural flavour.

The rules governing Armagnac were laid down in 1909, by which time the new vines, planted after the scourge of phylloxera in 1878 had wiped out all the original vineyards, were producing enough to be a commercial proposition. They now cover more than 12,000 hectares (30,000 acres) mostly in the Gers, together with some parishes in Lot-et-Garonne and Lande. There are technically three sections lying within the permitted zone of the *appellation d'origine*. Bas-Armagnac has a sandy, acid soil which they claim gives the brandy a smell of prunes and peaches. Haut-Armagnac, well to the east with fewer than 160 hectares (400 acres) of chalky land, has a small production, but the spirit from Ténarèze, which lies between the two, on a soil of clay and chalk mixed with sand, is possibly the most delicate, supposedly smelling of violets.

Not only is the region demarcated, but the type of grapes used in making the wine to distil, the methods and timing of distillation, and the ageing process in oak barrels are all carefully prescribed.

The grapes, usually Folle Blanche, Ugni Blanc or Colombard (although several others including Jurançon and Clairette de Gascogne are allowed), make a simple wine of high acidity but low alcoholic content, never more than 9° volume. The distillation is done quite soon after the *vendange*, so the acidity does not fade, and must by law be done before 31st March. Traditionally, distillation was done at 52.2°C, although the regulations permit temperatures of up to 70°C. The bigger commercial manufacturers lately have inclined to distil at a greater heat as this does eliminate more impurities and appears to make the spirit mature more quickly.

All Armagnac must mature in an oak cask for at least one year, when it can be sold labelled as three-star brandy. The labels VO, VSOP and Réserve mean that the least time any part of the blend of Armagnacs has been in the cask is four years. The rather generous terms Extra, Napoléon, XO and, even more suggestive of maturity, *Hors d'Age* and *Vieille Réserve*, mean only one more year. Of course, some better blends from respectable houses contain a handsome amount of older spirit, while others add a little older stuff, as one producer once put it to me, dropped in by a fly or with a fork, and hint at twenty years in the oak. By far the best are the vintage brandies, that have been aged in the wood for at least fifteen years and are not blended with any other year.

When newly distilled the alcohol content of Armagnac is very high. Over the years in the barrel it loses much of its strength, but spirit which has only been in the barrel a comparatively short time is too strong for sale. To bring it down to the standard 43°, they add what the manufacturers coyly refer to as their secret *petites eaux*, which is really to say water. This is forbidden in the case of vintage Armagnac. The first act of anyone testing a vintage Armagnac is to shake the bottle

Paul Dubourdieu's methods are hardly orthodox – he happily leaves his barrels out in all weathers, for instance. Yet somehow he manages to make an Armagnac fit not just for heroes, but for the gods.

vigorously. If it is genuinely pure, bubbles will linger for several seconds on the top of the brandy. If water has been added, they will vanish immediately.

There are no grand Armagnac houses to compare with, say, Hennessy, Courvoisier, or Rémy Martin in Cognac, and it is often the small, independent, *polyculture* farmer – that is to say the man who keeps a few cows and some sheep, grows a little corn for his ducks and his geese, and tends his vines to make the wine that he distills into Armagnac – who produces the best brandy.

A marvellous example is Paul Dubourdieu, an eccentric man of 63 who farms less than 40 hectares (100 acres) in Ténarèze near Mézin. The first time I went to his farm, I could not believe that anything of any quality could emerge from this complete shambles. A dead ram, on its back in a wheelbarrow, was swelling in the sun. A cow lay exhausted at the entrance to a tractor shed; she had plainly given birth in the night. Ducks and chickens wandered in a way for which the word free-range was an understatement. Old machinery rusted in spiked heaps. In front of the house stood the still, a Heath-Robinson affair that looked precisely in the right

André Daguin, the greatest of Gascon chefs, has preserved the Hôtel de France in Auch as a perfect nineteenth-century hotel, with every modern comfort. He uses the produce of his region – ducks, foie gras *and* Armagnac – *in a way that elevates even these delights beyond ordinary imagination.*

place. Barrels were strewn everywhere, some in long rows, others nearly hidden under trees, some indoors in a tall building, others seemingly abandoned among the elders and the tangled undergrowth.

Monsieur Dubourdieu's animals loved him and his face shone with pleasure at their affection. A calf trotted after him and he pretended to give it brandy from a bottle and fondled its testicles, laughing as he said, 'That's good, isn't it?'; a proud cockerel ate from a spoon he held out to it. It was easy to picture the scene a friend had described to me of a day when he went by chance to buy some brandy. It was the day for killing the pig on the farm, a day of intense activity. Just after they killed the pig, Dubourdieu's old mother died. There was nothing to be done; the pig that would feed them all year must be dealt with – the hams set to cure, the *boudins* made. It was out of the question to stop. So they laid Granny out on the table, next to where they were working, and got on with it.

The friend said that he found it rather beautiful in its naturalness and in the simple recognition of the fact that life must go on.

Then we tasted Dubourdieu's Armagnac. We sat at a long wooden table in a room as jumbled as the outside, a mad clutter of bits and pieces, reminding me of photographs of Edwardian rooms. Madame Dubourdieu brought glasses and with great deliberation poured us first three glasses of *Floc de Gascogne*, one red, one rosé and one white. *Floc* is an apéritif, made of the must or unfermented grape juice with a little Armagnac added, about as strong as sherry. This is made by their son, Bernard. Usually it is too sweet for my taste, but their white was excellent. Next we ate some prunes bottled in Armagnac and sipped a little *eau de vie de pruneau* which were both delightful. Then came the 1975 vintage Armagnac. Somehow out of the muddle of this time-arrested farm Dubourdieu, in defiance of all the accepted practices (although always within the *appellation* regulations), makes a brandy fit not just for heroes but for the gods.

I had hoped that Dubourdieu supplied that greatest of Gascon chefs, Albert Daguin of the Hôtel de France in Auch, as he had once supplied the Carlton in Cannes. The Hôtel de France is marvellously agreeable and its majestic dining-room with masses of space and high ceiling belongs to an almost forgotten age.

Daguin, in fact has several Armagnac suppliers, because he needs different brandies for different purposes, but through him we met another *polyculture* farmer, Jacques Théaux. Here was a very different farm. Some fine cedars and a droopy pine hung over the neat, ochre-coloured buildings and beyond the house was a pretty rose garden.

Jacques Théaux is a diffident man who walks with a pronounced limp. There is something pleasingly correct about him, though he has no trace of pomposity. His barrels are all kept in a storehouse built by his father in 1926. The temperature never rises in this dark place above 17°C, and never falls below 12°C. When I asked him about Dubourdieu's happily leaving barrels out in the sun or in the snow, he refused to condemn it though he was obviously shocked. He merely said that the heat would make for a huge loss of evaporation and that the changes of temperature would speed up the ageing process, which as it happens was exactly what Dubourdieu had said.

One of Daguin's suppliers is La Maison Marcel Trépout, whose cellars, built in 1135, are well worth a visit, if only for the ancient still.

Théaux produces only vintage Armagnac. His methods have not changed at all from his father's day, except that he no longer does his own distilling, but takes his wine to a new distillery not far away. There they distil at 54.2°C rather than the old 52.2°C in order to achieve the same taste, but, as Théaux points out, no two barrels ever taste precisely the same. He recites with pride the years in which vintage Armagnac has been made since the turn of the century. There are long gaps, for example from 1915 until 1932. Evidently the demand for Armagnac at that time was so small that the farmers made more money selling their wine as wine than they would have by distilling it. The late 1930s were barren years.

'I think things were difficult at that time, but I expect you know more about that than I do. And there was the war and that must have been a trouble.' Again, he thought that I might know more about it. But the vintage years coincided with the war years, coming to an abrupt end after 1946 and not resuming until 1959. But from 1962 onwards there has been a vintage every year.

Albert Daguin does not use Théaux' Armagnac in his cooking. For cooking he needs a younger brandy. 'What I want is the scent, not the alcohol – that disappears. In an old brandy the scent fades, while in younger ones it is drowned by the alcohol. I love cooking with Armagnac, but it isn't suitable for everything, because of this alcohol question. It must burn off, so that only the scent is left. This means a lot of heat which is not right for many things.'

Daguin's cuisine, as befits a Gascon, is richer than that of many trendier chefs, but one leaves his hotel with the feeling that one has enjoyed something that is genuinely French rather than the product of a dreary homogeneity. The first of his recipes, while not difficult to execute, may be hard in that fresh duck *foie gras* is not readily available everywhere. The second, which he discovered some fifteen years ago, is a treat that will make up for any disappointment.

Foie de canard frais à la julienne

FRESH DUCK *FOIE GRAS* WITH MIXED VEGETABLES

For 4

1 fresh duck *foie gras,* about 600 g (1 lb, 5 oz) in weight
2 carrots
2 large turnips
2 leeks
2 celery stalks
150 ml (5 fl oz) Armagnac
300 ml (10 fl oz) stock (preferably chicken)
salt and pepper

Trim and peel the vegetables as appropriate. Cut them into *julienne,* or very thin strips.

Discard the greenish part of the liver round the bile pocket. Pull out the main vein and skin the liver; never cut it open to take out the nerves. Marinate the liver for 3 hours in very salty iced water.

Preheat the oven to 180°C(350°F) Gas 4.

Make a bed of the vegetable *julienne* in the bottom of an appropriately sized terracotta oven dish. Lay the liver upside down on the top. Season with salt and pepper and the Armagnac. Cover and cook for 20 minutes in the preheated oven. Add the chicken stock, turn the liver over and cook for 10 minutes more.

Dish the liver and the vegetables on to a heated serving plate. Pour the sauce into a pan, and reduce until it thickens. Pour it over the liver. Take care that the fat coming out of the liver when you cut it does not curdle the sauce.

La glace aux pruneaux à l'Armagnac

PRUNE AND ARMAGNAC ICE CREAM

For 4
225 g (8 oz) pitted prunes
Armagnac to cover
Custard
10 egg yolks
250 g (9 oz) caster sugar
1 litre (1¾ pints) milk

Fill a jar with prunes and cover them completely with Armagnac. Seal the jar and leave the prunes to soak for 2-3 weeks. The prunes must never be cooked or heated at any time.

When ready to prepare the ice cream, make the custard. Beat the egg yolks and sugar together in an enamel bowl until the mixture is smooth and white. Meanwhile bring the milk to the boil three times. Pour this into the egg yolk mixture, beating all the time. Pour everything back into the pan you boiled the milk in and heat gently, still beating, until the custard is thick and coats the back of a wooden spoon. If it is overcooked and takes on the consistency of scrambled eggs, a spin in the blender will retrieve it. Let the custard cool in a bowl covered with muslin.

When cold, put the custard in the *sorbetière*. Slowly add the majority of the prunes (which will break up on their own) and the Armagnac they soaked in. Churn until frozen. The resulting ice cream should be creamy and smooth. Keep one prune for each guest by way of decoration.

If you do not have a *sorbetière*, whizz the prunes and Armagnac in the food processor or blender until in fine pieces. Stir into the custard and freeze in a suitable container. Stir every couple of hours until smooth.

Albert Daguin

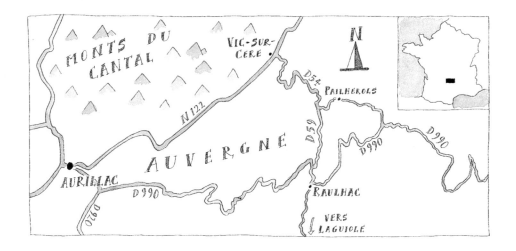

Cantal Cheese

The Auvergne is one of the most mysterious as well as the most diverse parts of France. At the lower altitudes, there are deep valleys with rushing rivers and streams bustling with trout. There are broad forests with fine stands of beech and oak. It is thinly populated and, to my mind, far more beautiful than anything the Dordogne or the Lot-et-Garonne has to offer, and it is so far unspoilt.

Higher up, there is the somehow sinister range of extinct volcanos known as Puys, several of them rising to more than 1,700 m (5,600 ft). The volcanic land around yields coal and the iron for the knife-makers of Laguiole and the scissor-makers of Thiers. As one goes up towards the mountains, the trees change to pines and higher still are rounded hills, bare of trees, but covered with grass where the cattle graze in the summer.

On just such a hillside in the Cantal region, we found Jules Porte milking his herd of cows by hand. He sat on a three-legged stool that was attached to the belt of his trousers, so that when he stood up to move to another cow, the stool went with him.

The cows were Salers, lovely chestnut-coloured creatures with thick furry coats and fine curved horns. There is much argument as to how this ancient breed of cattle compares with the equally ancient Aubrac (see the piece on beef). Despite their thicker skins, the Salers are not as hardy as the Aubrac, nor are they capable of being used as draught animals. Their meat has possibly not quite so full a flavour. On the other hand, what is unquestionable is the quality of their milk, which is used to make Cantal cheese.

Jules Porte tends this herd of 50 cows for the four months of the *transhumance*, when the cattle are brought up from the valleys to take advantage of the summer pastures in the mountains. There is no system such as that in Haute-Savoie, where the cattle owners lease their herds in the summer to mountain people, who graze the cows on common land and make Reblochon cheese and then give back the herd to the owners in September. Jules is a simple employee of the herd-owner, who also owns the land that Jules grazes them over.

When he had finished milking the cows and they had wandered off to graze, their cow-bells tinkling as if they were in a pastoral movie, Jules led us to his *buron*, a combination of a shepherd's hut and a cheese-making place. There are *burons* dotted all over the high lands of the Auvergne, and they are, for the most part, rough, low, stone buildings with long roofs of stone tiles, which might have been built at any time in the last 400 years. Jules' *buron* was a far superior building, almost grand enough to be called a house. Over its door there was even a date – 1906. At ground level there was one large room.

With the help of a friend, Jules brought in the afternoon's milk and poured it

Jules Porte is one of the last herders of Salers cattle who spend the summer up in the high pastures of the Auvergne, making their cheese in a traditional manner, milking by hand, and living four months in a buron *or rough shepherd's hut.*

M. Porte works on the curds by hand before putting them into a press overnight. There is nothing mechanical in this old-fashioned method of cheese-making.

into a tall barrel, drawing off a litre (1¾ pints) for his family's use. The cows each give about 8 litres (14 pints) of milk a day. As it takes 10 litres (17½ pints) of milk to make 1 kg (2¼ lb) of cheese, Jules makes a 40 kg (88 lb) cheese for every day of the *transhumance*.

Into the barrel of milk he poured a small amount of a cheese rennet extracted from calves' stomachs, as a *presure* or starter. While waiting for this to act, he took out from a press the block of pressed curds made from the morning's milking. He shredded this into a cradle, adding to it a bowlful of salt, and then took it below into the cellar.

After an hour, or three-quarters of an hour if the weather is hot, the milk in the barrel separates into curds and whey. Jules breaks up the curds with something that looks like a ski-stick. The whey is drawn off and ends up in a bath-tub in one corner of the room and is eventually fed to some pigs that Jules keeps behind the *buron*. The curds are put into a press overnight, shredded and then taken below to the cellar, where the temperature must never rise above 14°C. There the whole day's yield is formed into a round shape, wrapped in a cloth and put into a press, where it remains for 38 hours, the cloth being changed twice a day. After that, the cheese is left to mature for a minimum of two months, but Jules says that the longer it is left, the better it is.

It sounds simple, but a lot depends on the timing of each step being exactly right. And this is more a question of instinct and of watching minutely the condition of the milk, the curds and the cheese at each stage, rather than of following a set timetable. For Jules it is second nature. 'I started when I was fourteen, so it has been a whole lifetime. In the old days, I used to live in the *buron* for all of the four months and come down only once a week at the most.'

Jules is a craftsman and his Cantal is superb, tasting completely different from anything I had ever had before. Factory-made Cantal is, to my taste, a rather dull cheese, but his is alive and rich, with a perfect texture. But it seems that we have not much time left to enjoy the real thing.

Jules has two sons. I asked him whether they would follow him, as he had followed his father and grandfather. His sharp, blue eyes saddened. 'No, there is no future. It ends with us, the few of us who are left.' It is the usual story. The EC regulations make his kind of private production impossible. To conform to all the absurd rules is economically impossible and would, in any case, change the nature of the cheese.

André Combourieu, who runs the Auberge des Montagnes in the tiny mountain village of Pailherols, takes an equally gloomy view of the future. 'These norms of the EC will kill everything, by making everything the same. Their terrible uniformity is going to destroy all the skills of the artisan.'

André, an energetic man of 40, with a smallish, round head, a domed forehead and very straight hair, has the look of an intellectual rather than a hotelier and chef. He has an impressive breadth of interests, being a person of intelligent curiosity. He will discourse upon design or geology or the charms of ski-ing. At the same time, he is by nature a great traditionalist. The Combourieu family has run the Auberge for four generations. 'My great-grandmother was both a cook and a couturier. My grandmother was a first-rate cook, who specialised in cooking

M. Porte produces a 40 kg (88 lb) cheese every day for four months. The result is a cheese so far removed from factory-made Cantal that you would not guess that the two products were in any way connected.

game. My father never cooked, but concentrated more on the running of the hotel.'

André's father, Jean, is still very much alive, but is fortunate to be so at all. During the war, as a young man in his early twenties, he was rounded up by the Germans, who wanted to revenge some act of the Resistance. He was put up against the wall to be shot. As the firing squad raised their guns, the Maquis created a sudden diversion. In the confusion, Jean managed to run away and hide himself in a field of rye.

André, like Jules, started work at the age of fourteen. One way and another, he learned his craft in Brittany, Lyon and Paris. But when he came back home and took over the kitchens of the Auberge, he was determined to keep to the local dishes of the Auvergne and particularly the area of Cantal.

The locals have appetites that belong to another age. André says he has lightened the dishes to cater for modern taste, yet most people would still find them filling, to put it at the mildest. As you may judge from his recipes, even with a salad, a fair amount of flour and a good bit of sausage find their way into almost any dish.

We should be glad that in this out-of-the-way corner the old standards remain. And no doubt those large numbers of enthusiastic British walkers who flock to this charming inn in the summer can work up the appetite to do justice to André's splendid cooking, enhanced by Jules Porte's cheese.

Tourtes au Cantal

CANTAL PIES

For 4
500 g (18 oz) puff pastry
1 egg yolk
Filling
20 g (¾ oz) butter
20 g (¾ oz) plain flour
250 ml (8 fl oz) milk
salt and pepper
150 g (5 oz) sausagemeat, crumbled
100 g (4 oz) young Cantal cheese, diced
100 g (4 oz) cooked ham, diced

For the filling, make a béchamel sauce. Melt the butter in a pan, add the flour, and let cook for a minute or two. Add the boiling milk, stirring continuously until taken up by the flour. Let simmer for 3 minutes, then season with salt and pepper. Cover with butter paper and let cool.

When cool, add the crumbled sausagemeat and cheese and ham dice. Mix well.

Preheat the oven to 220°C (425°F) Gas 7.

Roll out the pastry and cut into eight circles of about 15 cm (6 in) in diameter. Divide the filling between four of the circles, leaving a narrow margin. Moisten these margins with some of the egg yolk. Cover each with the remaining circles, and press down well to seal. Paint with the remaining egg yolk, and transfer to a baking sheet. Bake in the preheated oven for about 20–25 minutes until puffed and golden.

Salade Cantalouse

CANTAL SALAD

For 4
320 g (11 oz) young Cantal cheese
80 g (3¼ oz) plain flour
2 large eggs, beaten
150 g (5 oz) dry breadcrumbs
about 2 tablespoons olive oil
1 lettuce
about 50 ml (2 fl oz) light French dressing
1 smoked sausage, sliced

Cut the cheese into squares of 5 cm (2 in) and 1 cm (½ in) thick. Roll them first in the flour and then in the beaten egg. Coat with the breadcrumbs. Fry in the olive oil until golden on both sides. Drain well on absorbent paper.

Separate the lettuce into leaves and dress with the French dressing.

On individual plates, make a bed of the dressed leaves and top with the warm, crisp cheese and some sausage slices.

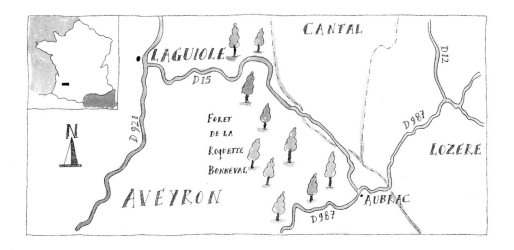

Beef

It was not until the 1840s that any serious effort was made to regulate or improve the beef livestock of France. Curiously, the spur was the importation of animals from Britain where the classification of the various breeds had been largely settled in the eighteenth century. British cattle, the Durham in particular, developed much more rapidly to the point when they were ready to be butchered.

These foreign animals found it hard to adapt, so the French set about classifying their own beef breeds and seeing what could be done to improve them. Gradually three breeds emerged as the most useful, partly because they were the best suited to the bigger commercial systems of breeding, which follow naturally from the general concept of classified breeds. These were Charolais, Limousin and Blonde d'Aquitaine, bred in regions of France such as the Morvan that, up until the Second Empire (1852-70) had been cereal country, and that in the last part of the nineteenth century became grazing land.

As the twentieth century progressed, with efficient transport, improved communications, and widespread advertising, the dominance of these breeds increased. In the last few years, however, a note of dissatisfaction has crept in. Bernard Loiseau, whose restaurant is in the heart of Charolais country, asks, 'What can one do that is interesting with a lump of meat?' The current fashion for excessively tender meat, with virtually no fat, has meant that taste has been sacrificed in favour of softness. Lucien Conquet, a butcher in Laguiole, grumbled to me that Limousin is not meat any longer, as it has been bred so that it cuts like

Paul Mathieu and his nephew with Faience, the prize Aubrac bull. This race of cattle is hardy, economical to keep, and delicious to eat. Overleaf: The hillsides of this part of the Auvergne are covered in summer with rich grasses: the gentian gives the milk a distinct taste, and the liquorice flavours the meat.

butter and tastes of nothing.

The reaction against artifical blandness has resulted in a revival of interest in a few ancient breeds that have been left purer because they are natives of remote areas less tightly knit with the general economy. Aubrac and Salers in the Auvergne and Tarine in the Alps are cases in point. Salers we look at in a different context (see page 58), and I incline to think that Aubrac is the best beef to be found in France today.

Paul Mathieu's farm is a large building of grey and white volcanic stone, the stones so set that they have the look of a mosaic. The original part dates from 1290. M. Mathieu is proud of two doorways that have a crusader's arms carved on the lintel. He also showed us a fireplace he recently uncovered that has over it a fresco dating, experts have told him, from the time of Louis XIV, but the main part of the house is eighteenth century.

There is an air of solidity and continuity about Lhon (*patois* for elm), as the farm is called, that matches both the farmer and his cattle. Mathieu is a stout man dressed in a boiler suit, round which he wears a belt. Above his round face, he wears a beret that he doffs with grave courtesy when greeting anyone, revealing

short, grey hair, and giving emphasis to his huge ear lobes which droop almost as much as his moustache.

When first we met him, he was hushed with shyness, which may account for his being unexpectedly a bachelor. He was sure that he would have nothing to say that could possibly interest us. But when we sat with him in his large kitchen, hung with copper pans, pictures of prize bulls and stuffed heads, and lit by lights mounted on old ox-yokes, his enthusiasm was captivating.

He had rented Lhon more than 30 years before and had managed to buy it eighteen years later. Over that time, he has built up his herd of Aubrac to the point where he is recognised as the leading breeder of pedigree bulls, although he did not make this claim for himself.

'Aubrac is a very old race, descended from bison and much purer than other races. It is a very strong strain. Even after they have been crossed with other cattle they always throw back to the pure Aubrac. They are lively and intelligent and if you call them by name they will always reply.'

When we went round the farm and the pastures with Mathieu, this proved to be so. When he called them, some would come to him and others would grunt to show that they were listening.

Aubrac, despite their size, are very gentle cattle, and M. Mathieu's are almost like pets, each one answering to its name with an amiable grunt.

The females are very different from the males, being paler and with none of the black that marks the shoulders and face of the bulls.

Mathieu listed the advantages of the breed. In the first place, they work very well which, before the coming of tractors, was their principal role. Of course they were kept also for milk and for meat, but it is only lately that beef has become their primary purpose. Their meat, he maintains, is unsurpassed – it is red and not too fat, but sufficiently marbled with fat to make it less dry. The taste is wonderful.

Furthermore they are economical creatures. In the winter when they are indoors, they eat only hay, no cattle cake, although I suspect he feeds them a few roots if the spring and early summer have been too dry to produce enough hay.

They have other useful characteristics that Mathieu did not list, perhaps fearful of wearying us with technical details – an amazing fecundity, a short calving interval, an ability to calve without help and a convenient calving pattern which means that all the calves are born within the first three months of the year, at a time when the cows are indoors.

We discussed the relative merits of Aubrac and Salers, the other ancient breed from the Auvergne that is now primarily bred for cheese-making (see page 58), but is considered by some to furnish good beef.

'Salers has a very thick skin which makes for poor meat, while the skin of an Aubrac is as thin as a cigarette paper. It is also not such a healthy animal. The Aubrac is far hardier and much more powerful. There are many Aubrac still working as draught animals but the Salers are just not strong enough.'

Lhon spreads over 150 hectares (375 acres), the land rising steeply behind the farmhouse to the rounded, close-grazed pastures of the volcanic plateau, some 1,100 m (3,630 ft) above sea level. Not far from the house lies a rather strange stone, half-carved with the face of a Madonna. It was worked by the previous owner of the farm, a devout man prevented by piety from finishing his task, when he realised that a flaw in the rock would look like a scar on the Virgin's face.

Mathieu used to employ ten men in earlier times, when he did both dairy and beef. Now, apart from a few potatoes, he sticks only to his herd. By way of a partner he has had, for six years, a young cousin, André, who was brought up on a farm where his parents kept Charolais, but who preferred the interest of a pure-bred herd.

Mathieu uses 70 hectares (175 acres) for grazing and the remaining 80 hectares (200 acres) for hay, which he cuts in July. This land, high above the wooded valleys and rushing streams of the region, has something of the same primitive feeling as the downs of Wessex. The wild plants play an important part in the life of his herd. The herbs, he says, are healthy – the gentian gives a rich taste to the milk and the liquorice flavours the meat.

The herd spends six months of the year out in the open, from 15th May until 15th November. Mathieu's cattle are beautiful to look at, a lovely, honey colour with darker patches, and this is a matter of pride for him, because his aim in building his herd was to make them handsome and uniform in appearance – 'like making a family'. It is also commercially sound, because a buyer can see at a glance the standard of what he is buying.

Mathieu has 80 cows and, of course, knows the name of every one, and can recite the pedigree of some of them back to 1946. The young heifers are sold at 30 months, which is late by the standards of other breeds, but Aubrac are slow developers. He believes that it is important never to push the animals too hard for fear of destroying what he calls their rusticity. Possibly for this reason he also never uses artificial insemination, but allows his bulls to mount naturally. The preservation of the breed is of prime importance to Mathieu. He achieves it so well that his herd is regarded as a model of purity. A large proportion of his young bulls, ten or a dozen every year, are sold for breeding.

His Aubrac bulls are majestic creatures, much darker than the cows, their heads and chests being nearly black, a difference emphasised by their lips, which are pure white. When he brought Faience, for eight years his prize bull, into the yard for us to admire, we were conscious of the primitive power of this huge beast. It was easy to identify him with a bison. Mathieu made us take our cars out of the yard, in case Faience, who had been roaming on the pasture land for many months, should feel frisky. But Faience was almost absurdly gentle, lumbering inquisitively towards us until Mathieu called to him to stop.

The bull wandered round the cobbled yard pausing to drink from the four vast stone troughs that sit in the middle. Mathieu told us that when Faience went to Paris for an agricultural show, he refused to drink the water there. All he drank in two weeks were the 10 litres (21 pints) they had set off with for the journey.

Lhon lies about 5 km (3 miles) from the town of Laguiole. Tell any Frenchman that you are going there and he will ask you to bring him back a knife. Nearly every shop in the place sells knives, ranging from small penknives to enormous blades costing £2,000 or more. It is logical because this volcanic region is rich in minerals – iron ore and the coal with which to smelt it. But this is not the only thing at which Laguiole excels. There is M. Conquet the butcher, who has won many prizes for the best sausages in France and, above all, there is Michel Bras – one of perhaps half a dozen or more young French chefs, who are intent on rescuing French *haute cuisine* from the homogeneous commercialism imposed on it by the last generation.

Much of the beef that Bras buys comes originally from Mathieu, but it is not practical for a restaurant to buy a whole carcass, so he buys through Lucien Conquet. A part of the young chef's determination is to preserve regional differences and for that reason it is natural for Michel Bras to use Aubrac, but there are other good reasons as well.

'It is a breed adapted to our climate and to our herbage. It is by nature not too fat and it has an inimitable taste. The luxury trade, eating modern Charolais, has forgotten the taste of beef.'

Exactly what he buys will depend on the dish it is intended for – either young heifers of 30 months, which according to Mathieu have a quite different taste, or animals about four or five years old which have had one calf. Conquet explains that one can never expect fashionable tenderness with Aubrac, because the grain of the meat is much smaller. It is interesting from a butcher's point of view that one has far greater wastage with Aubrac than with other breeds. 'I can use 70 per cent of a Blonde d'Aquitaine, but only 55 per cent of an Aubrac. It may sound uneconomic, but then you can keep three Aubrac on the space needed for two Charolais. Anyhow I am only interested in the taste.'

Michel Bras has firm views on the cooking of meat. First, he wants to know how it has been killed. If a beast has a stressful death, its muscles will have become tense and the meat will be tough. Then he wants to know that it has been properly hung for three weeks.

'Meat should always be cooked well in advance. Start fast to seal the meat, then cook slowly, the slower the better. And then the meat must be allowed to relax.'

The result, in his care, is astonishing. It is true that one has forgotten, too, that having to bite is not such a disaster. It is not that Aubrac is tough; it is merely agreeably firm. The recipe for a *bavette* (top of the sirloin) reflects Michel Bras' passion for vegetables and grains. When he gave it to me to eat, he included among the seeds some *quinoa*, the grain of the Incas, said to be the most nourishing cereal in the world. He produced also a list of 199 vegetables that he likes to use in his cooking. At that rate, it is not surprising that he changes his menu every day. His other recipe, also demonstrating his love of wild flowers, is there simply because I thought it delicious and unfamiliar.

His restaurant is up in the hills near Lhon, so that one can eat gazing out over Paul Mathieu's pastures. It is hard to imagine a greater pleasure.

La bavette poêlée sur un jus aux céréales fermentées, graines germées

BRAISED SIRLOIN OF BEEF ON A SAUCE OF
FERMENTED CEREALS WITH SPROUTING
SEEDS

For 4

1 thick cut, about 800 g (1¾ lb) in weight, from
the top of the sirloin
225 g (8 oz) in all of lentils, soya beans, wheat
grains, lucerne seeds, etc, already germinated
(see below)
15 g (½ oz) pearl barley
60 ml (2¼ fl oz) red wine
60 ml (2¼ fl oz) sweet white wine (from
Banyuls)
1 teaspoon Dijon mustard
20 g (¾ oz) *miso* paste (fermented soya bean
paste)
30 g (1¼ oz) unsalted butter
2 teaspoons olive oil
salt and pepper

The sauce: The day before you wish to cook,
soak the pearl barley in cold water overnight.

In the morning, drain the barley, pat it
dry, and grill it in a frying pan with no fat
until it is brown. Put the barley in water
again (5 measures of water to one of barley)
and boil for 30–45 minutes. Drain, but keep
the water.

In another pan, boil and reduce by two-
thirds the red wine and sweet white wine.
Add the mustard, *miso* paste and the grilled,
drained barley. Mix thoroughly and, if the
sauce is too thick, add a little of the barley
cooking water.

The meat: Cut the piece of meat against the
grain into four equal parts, discarding the
nerves and any skin. Season the pieces of
meat with salt. Place them in a very hot frying pan, greased with 10 g (¼ oz) of the butter and the oil. Sauté to seal in the juices until
brown (2 minutes on each side). Lower the

heat and carry on cooking for 1 minute on
each side. This is the correct cooking time
for pieces of meat about 2 cm (¾ in) thick,
and weighing about 150–175 g (5-6 oz) each.

When cooked, put aside in a warm place
to give the fibres a chance to relax.

To serve: Heat the barley sauce, then slide in
the remaining butter and stir slowly over
heat to warm through, finally adding the
juices from the meat. Season to taste.

Spoon a little of the warm sauce on to the
side of each plate. Season the meat with salt
and pepper, and arrange on the sauce. Display the different germinated seeds harmo-
niously on the other side of the plate, and
serve.

Some newly sprouted seeds, grains and
pulses can be bought in good
supermarkets. It is easy to do this at
home. Special sprouters are available, or
use a large jar, some muslin and an elastic
band.

Three days at least in advance, soak the
lentils and other chosen cereals and seeds
in water for several hours, then drain.
Place in sprouter or jars, separately; cover
the tops of the jars with the muslin and
fix with the elastic band. Place in a dark,
even temperature place, and rinse night
and morning for a couple of days. The
grains and seeds are ready when
germination begins, when the skins crack
and the first shoots appear.

Les fruits rouges, semoule et crème glacée à la reine des prés

RED FRUIT, SEMOLINA AND MEADOWSWEET ICE CREAM

For 4

400g (14 oz) red fruit (strawberries, wild
strawberries, red, white and black currants,
raspberries, blackberries, bilberries)
40 g (1½ oz) granulated sugar
Ice cream
a bunch of fresh meadowsweet flowers
350 ml (12 fl oz) milk
5 egg yolks
60 g (2¼ oz) granulated sugar
85 ml (3 fl oz) UHT cream
Semolina
50 ml (2 fl oz) milk
1 tablespoon UHT cream
15 g (½ oz) granulated sugar
20 g (¾ oz) unsalted butter
20 g (¾ oz) white semolina
1 egg, separated

The ice cream: Stew most of the meadow-sweet flowers for 5 minutes in the boiling milk. Filter through a fine sieve.

Beat the egg yolks and sugar together. Add the perfumed milk gradually, mixing well, to make a custard. Stir constantly over a gentle heat to a thick consistency, then pour in the cream. Filter again, then leave to cool for several hours.

Pour into a *sorbetière* and blend until smooth and thick. Or pour into a freezer container and freeze, stirring well every couple of hours until smooth.

The fruit: Wash and drain the fruit well, discarding stems and leaves. Separate the fruits from each bunch. Roll them in granulated sugar.

The semolina: Mix together the milk, cream, sugar and butter in a pan, then bring to the boil. Sprinkle in the semolina and whip the mixture over a gentle heat. Remove from the heat, cover, and leave to allow the mixture to expand for 10 minutes. Add the egg yolk, mix in well, then leave to cool.

Beat the egg white and fold it gently into the semolina. Put aside.

Either use eight tiny circular moulds, 4.5 cm (1¾ in) in diameter and 3 cm (1¼ in) high, or make eight paper cylinders to the same dimensions from greaseproof paper.

Arrange the moulds or cylinders in a hot non-stick frying pan and pour some of the semolina mixture into each one to a depth of 5 mm (¼ in). Cook on a slow heat until bubbles appear on the top. Take the mould or paper off, and turn the cakes over. Cook for 4 minutes more and put aside in a warm place.

To serve: Arrange the fruit on four dessert plates. Put two semolina cakes on top. Spoon some of the meadowsweet ice cream over the cakes. Decorate the plate with the reserved fresh meadowsweet flowers.

Michel Bras

Meadowsweet (*Filipendula ulmaria*) is a damp-loving flowering herb, also known as meadwort and queen of the meadow (*reine des prés*). The creamy white flowers smell sweet, like honey and almonds, and they are used in folk medicine. The flowers appear from midsummer, but are also available dried. If you cannot find meadowsweet, you could flavour the ice cream with honey.

Truffles

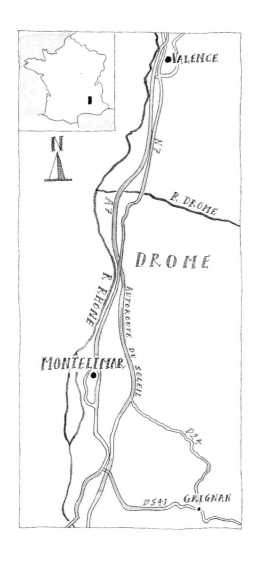

The castle of Grignan stands proud above the little town, looking out over the vineyards of the Côte du Rhône. It was here that Madame de Sevigné wrote her famous letters. In those days, the landscape was little different from what it is today, but it has, since her time, been through various changes.

When the scourge of phylloxera struck at the end of the last century, the farmers ripped out their useless vines and planted fine stands of oak, rather as they had done some years before when the south-east of France suffered terrible floods and they had planted trees to hold the land together. In the winter, from under these trees, the local people gathered amazing quantities of truffles.

Gradually, however, the farmers reverted to their traditional wine-growing. The trees were cut down and the gathering of truffles was much reduced. Today, the total production of truffles in France is little more than 100 tons a year, whereas in 1900 it amounted to 1,000 tons.

Round Grignan, there are still people who live by producing truffles, although producing is hardly the word because, as we shall see, the truffle is a whimsical, intractable thing, not susceptible of cultivation. Among them is Pierre Aymé, a good-looking man in his late forties, who has 12 hectares (30 acres) of land beside the River Lez, of which 10.5 (26¼ acres) are given over to the hope of truffles.

The French edible truffle, *Tuber melanosporum*, is commonly known as the Périgord truffle. It is, incidentally, apart from the *Tuber magnatum* (the delicious, highly scented, Italian white truffle), the only truffle with any gastronomic merit. The so-called summer truffle (*T. aestivum*) which does appear in England, especially in the New Forest, is a pointless thing. Despite the name, however,

Périgord is by no means the most productive area for truffles. Both the Drôme and the Vaucluse claim to be the most important source of this strangest and most mysterious of all the things we eat.

Truffles have been known and prized from the earliest times. They have, perhaps because of their elusive nature, been the subject of many myths. Pliny said that they did not spring from any seed, but were the offspring of storms. Plutarch, who lived not far away at the Fontaine de Vaucluse, believed they were not vegetable at all, but were composed of a mixture of earth and minerals. His theory did not stop his eating them.

In the nineteenth century, the beliefs were just as wild. The Abbé Charvat was convinced that they grew somehow out of dust on the leaves of oak trees washed down by the rain, and another expert was of the opinion that truffles were growths on the roots of trees, produced by bites from an insect.

Almost everything to do with truffles presents difficulties or puzzles. They grow usually under oak or hazelnut trees, but it is no good planting these trees and just hoping. There must be, though no-one yet has managed to identify them, other essential factors. Presumably the quality of the soil plays a large part, as they grow only in limited areas. The individual trees themselves must have an influence, for it is perfectly possible for one tree to have an abundance of truffles beneath its spread, while a tree of identical appearance, only 6 m (20 ft) away, will have none. Pierre says that under one tree he will always find big truffles, while another will only ever shelter small ones. There is no obvious reason why.

People have spent fortunes trying to find ways of ensuring that truffles will grow. Every few years there is a great flurry as someone is said to have discovered the answer, but nothing happens. As Pierre points out, 'We now are told that the Japanese have managed to reproduce the scent of the truffle in a laboratory, but who has seen it or smelled it?' In the right areas, there is a reasonable chance that, if you plant a grove of oaks, you will in time have truffles, but there are not many people willing to give up good land, knowing that at the very least they will have to wait fifteen years before they see any return.

The next problem is to find them. There are three possible ways of locating truffles. The first is to use a pig to hunt for them. Pigs are the best searchers and easy to train, but they have disadvantages. One is that they are greedily fond of truffles and are inclined to gobble them up before the owner can get them. Another is that they grow fat and uncontrollable, so that you have to have a new pig every year.

The second method of finding truffles is tricky and requires a certain knowledge of where the truffles might lie. There is usually no vegetation under a tree that encourages truffles. The method is to gaze across a likely bare piece of earth, looking towards the sun and watch out for a particular kind of pale fly which dances up and down over a truffle.

The most practical method is to use a dog. They can be trained to like truffles. Pierre has five. He starts early with his puppies, by rubbing truffle butter on the mother's nipples. 'We always love what we eat as children, even if it is bad like fast food.' The dogs are not of any particular breed: 'I would describe them as pedigree mongrels.' The relationship between the dog and his master must be very close, 'My father's best dog, for example, died within a month of his death.'

Dogs, however, are expensive. Rita, Pierre's favourite, is now twelve years old, but even at that age is still worth £3,000. Her daughter, Roxanne, is so far a little uncertain, but will one day, he believes, be just as good as her mother.

We went out into the woods with Pierre and it was fascinating to see the dogs work. Within a minute, Rita had found something, and scratched at the earth. Pierre went over and, with a metal rod, he dug down and picked out a truffle the size of a golf ball. He uses the rod to expose the truffle because, if it was not yet big enough to be worth taking, and he touched it with his hand, it would rot in the ground. The dogs work best at about ten o'clock in the morning, when the distracting scents of the nocturnal rabbits, hares and rats have faded.

The growth cycle of the truffle is quite strange. It seems that in May there may be 80 potential truffles in a square metre or yard, joined in some way to the tree that is their host, but only a small number survive. In the middle of June, this umbilical link is severed and the truffle grows independently, anything up to 30 cm (1 ft) below the surface. They continue to grow right through the year and until March or April of the following year.

Pierre says that all they need in that time is water and warmth. Ideally, there should be a little rain every month. A drought is fatal. One can start searching for them in November, but the full flavour and scent of the truffle does not develop for some time, usually until there has been a frost. Pierre thinks that they are at their best after Christmas, around 10th to 15th January. One can go on looking for them well into March, but by that time they will have become very black, and the pale veins running through the truffle, which hold a good part of the scent, will have been crushed by the blacker flesh.

Truffles may vary in size from ones like that found by Rita or even smaller, to things as big as a cricket ball or occasionally larger. 'My father was proud of the biggest one he ever found, which weighed 120 grams [4¼ oz]. I was lucky enough to find an even larger one of 650 grams [nearly 1½ lb] but my son, in his turn, has found an immense one of 820 grams [over 1¾ lb].'

The whole business is so unpredictable. 'One hopes to get something between 12 and 15 kilos [26-33 lb] a year from each hectare, but in 1990, for example, I did not get even as much as one kilo per hectare.'

If all goes well, the truffles can produce a reasonable income. The price Pierre can expect is between £300 and £400 a kilogram (2¼ lb). In a moderately good year he might make £40,000, but in a year like 1990 he would get only £2-3,000.

Pierre Aymé, with two of his five dogs. The winter, preferably after January 10, is the best time to hunt for truffles. It's a precarious profession, because there is no way of guaranteeing that a crop will grow.

As if the hazards of nature are not enough, Pierre has human dangers to contend with. Last New Year's Day, he went out to find that poachers had come in the night and made 59 holes, presumably stealing the same number of truffles. He was convinced that they had not even used a torch. But then I have heard stories of poachers whose dogs are trained to go into the woods and dig up truffles which they bring to their thieving owners, who wait safely by their cars on the road.

To confuse the issue further, there is an ancient mystique about the selling of truffles, most of which goes on in various market towns. Outsiders have little hope of buying in a market. I have been told that there are no truffles to be had, or been directed to a back street and shown a few doubtful-looking nobbles, possibly with a few bits of lead pushed in under the skin to increase the weight, for which an enormous price was asked. All dealings are conducted in whispers, strictly for cash.

Pierre is in a more regular way of business. Most of his truffles are preserved and sold in jars. Ordinarily, a fresh truffle will keep its full flavour and scent for only a week. They can be frozen, but that again means using them quickly, and frozen ones are better cooked rather than used raw in salads. The only good way of preserving them is to put them in a jar with salt, seal it, and then boil the jar for 1½-3½ hours in a *bain-marie*, until the contents boil.

His fresh truffles he used to sell to Jacques Pic, the famous restaurateur at Valence, who sadly died last year. It is here that the last mystery of the truffle raises its head. What does a truffle do for cuisine? Why has it been a delicacy for so many

The sale of truffles is often conducted in great secrecy. In some parts of France, old Roman measures are still used to weight the 'black diamonds'.

centuries and for so many different palates? How does it manage to inspire Colette to write about it in such extravagant terms: 'that most capricious and most revered of black princesses'?

I talked to Jacques Pic about truffles not long before he died. He was always more than generous with them in his cuisine and, from so distinguished a chef, his practical tribute was, in its way, even more fulsome than any literary praise. He used at least 200 truffles a month in his inspired kitchens and in the course of a year probably spent £50–60,000 on them alone.

The truffle's magic, I learned from him, lies not just in its own taste and exotic aroma, but in its ability to bring out and enhance the taste of other things. A chicken cooked with slivers of truffle under its skin is so much more of a chicken than it would ordinarily be.

In the days of abundance, it was thought grand to cover anything and everything with slices of truffle. But with Jacques Pic, however lavish he may have been, one was conscious that he used his truffles for a real gastronomic reason. The death of Jacques Pic was a grievous tragedy, because no more agreeable and honourable man ever existed. The only slight consolation is that his son Alain will carry on the family tradition, doubtless using Pierre's truffles to the same glorious purpose.

We may judge some of these purposes from the recipes from the Restaurant Pic, devised by father and son. But these odd tubers have amazing effects of all sorts. A truffle permeates whatever it comes in contact with. If, overnight, you put some eggs into a closed pot with a truffle and, in the morning, boil or scramble the eggs they will be the best you have ever tasted.

Pierre Gleize keeps a huge truffle in a large jar full of *Marc de Provence*, and lets it sit for four years. The result is a brandy of unforgettable richness, smooth, earthy and delicately scented all at the same time.

The last word must rest with the nineteenth-century gastronome-poet, Monselet, who gave his name to many dishes using artichoke hearts, although artichokes were not his dearest love. 'I would like to be buried,' he said, '*aux truffes.*'

Truffes de la Drôme en cocotte de pomme de terre

TRUFFLES IN POTATO NESTS

For 4

5 fresh truffles (or whole canned with their
juices), about 25 g (1 oz) each
4 new potatoes
300 g (11 oz) broad bean pods
2 carrots, peeled and cut into four
2 small turnips, peeled and cut into four
500 g (18 oz) asparagus, trimmed
200 g (7 oz) butter
juice of 1 lemon
salt and pepper

Peel the potatoes and cut off one-third to
form a hat, and hollow out the rest to form a
'nest'. Blanch both nests and hats in boiling
water. Drain well.

Shell the beans, blanch in boiling salted
water, then pop the bright green beans out
of their skins. If you like, 'turn' or carve the
carrot and turnip pieces into oval shapes.

Lightly cook the asparagus, carrot and
turnip separately in salted water. Season
them and then cook lightly in a frying pan
with 25 g (1 oz) of the butter. Fry the
potatoes as well until golden. Reserve in a
warm place.

In a pan, boil 100 ml (3½ oz) water with
salt, pepper and the lemon juice, then take
off the heat. Beat in the remaining butter to
obtain a buttery foam. Cut one of the truffles
in half; slice one half, and finely dice the
other. Add both to the butter sauce.

Briefly heat up the remaining four truffles
in the butter sauce. Stuff each potato with a
warmed truffle. Place on the serving plate
and display the vegetables around. Pour the
butter sauce over, and serve.

Charlotte de dorade aux aubergines

BREAM AND AUBERGINE CHARLOTTE

For 10

2 bream, about 800 g (1¾ lb) each, cleaned,
skinned and filleted
3 kg (7 lb) aubergines, washed and trimmed
50 ml (2 fl oz) olive oil
5 tomatoes
salt and pepper
Sauce
100 g (4 oz) shallots, peeled and sliced
1 kg (2¼ lb) fennel bulbs, trimmed and sliced
(keep the frondy leaves)
200 g (7 oz) butter
250 ml (8 fl oz) white wine
1 litre (1¾ pints) fish stock, boiled to reduce to a
quarter
1 litre (1¾ pints) *crème fraîche*
a little Pernod or Ricard (*pastis*)

Slice the aubergines into a colander. Salt and
let drain, about 30 minutes. Fry the slices in
most of the oil until soft and golden, then let
them cool and drain on absorbent paper.

Cut the fish fillets in pieces. Cube the
tomatoes and fry in the remaining olive oil.

Place ten flan rings measuring 8 cm (3¼ in)
on a sheet of greaseproof paper on a baking
tray. Line each ring with a thick layer of
aubergine, covering the bottom and sides.
Fill the middle with the fish and tomatoes.
Finish with a topping of aubergine and seal
with another sheet of greaseproof paper.

For the sauce, fry the shallots and fennel in
50 g (2 oz) of the butter until soft, then add
the wine, the reduced fish stock, *crème fraîche*
and Pernod. Blend all ingredients in a liqui-
diser or blender, then sieve. Beat the remaining butter in, in small pieces, then season to
taste. Keep warm.

Steam the charlottes for 8 minutes.

Pour the sauce into the middle of each
serving plate. Unmould a charlotte into the
middle and decorate with the fennel leaves.

Jacques and Alain Pic

Vegetables

A significant part of the new spirit abroad in the world of French cuisine is the importance attached to vegetables. Formerly, vegetables were seen very much as ancillary to the main ingredient of a dish. Lately they have been, as it were, upgraded to a primary status.

Some of the enterprising young chefs, passionate about the produce of their region, go out into the fields and search for wild plants for their salads, or herbs to give flavour to their cooking. A great many top-class chefs such as Marc Meneau and Pierre Gleize have their own vegetable gardens. Michel Bras (see the piece on beef) is so fascinated by vegetables that he showed me a list of nearly 200 different kinds that he likes to work with. Bernard Loiseau, the newest of the Michelin three-star restaurateurs (see the piece on snails), actually has a vegetarian menu.

This new consciousness is not confined to restaurants, but also has an environmental element about it. Every Saturday morning, down a narrow side street at the market in Apt in the Vaucluse, Jean-Luc Daneyrolles, an unexpectedly good-looking young man, has a stall at which he sells the unusual vegetables and fruit that he grows on a plot of land he rents some 8 km (5 miles) outside the town.

Strange curling gourds, red, orange, yellow and white tomatoes, physalis or what we call Cape gooseberries, orache, a kind of wild spinach, Jerusalem artichokes (despised by the French because they were often the only vegetable to be had during the war), black potatoes with violet flesh (though I don't think much of those), yellow beetroot, parsnips, rare parsleys, purple basil, even rhubarb which most French people have never heard of.

Jean-Luc is something of a botanist, knowing the history of many of the

Jean-Luc Daneyrolles is almost more of a botanist than a market gardener. He is passionate about preserving old varieties of vegetable, and much of his produce (overleaf) has an exotic and colourful appearance. He has taught himself the botanical name of each plant and its history.

vegetables he grows: for instance that Cape gooseberries came originally from Peru, not, as many imagine, from South Africa. There is a crusading aspect to his labours. 'I want to see that the old vegetables that many people have forgotten are not lost forever.' A virtually self-educated man, he grapples with Latin and foreign names and loves the old French names – for example *laitue blanche paresseuse* ('lazy white lettuce') and he has a passion for accuracy. He was much upset that in the film *Manon des Sources* they used the wrong kind of marrow.

Jean-Luc's interests are diverse, but mostly concerned with the past. 'I live more in the past than in the future.' He is proud of his bit of land, which he tends with affectionate care, believing, for instance, that ploughing disturbs the soil. On it, he has found Stone-age axe heads, and he likes to speculate about the old road nearby. Was it originally Roman, for there was a Roman villa just by his boundary?

Of necessity, Jean-Luc sells some of his produce to restaurants, 'although I am

not happy that they treat them with the respect they deserve.' Nor were we happy that any restaurants in the gastronomic desert round Apt were worthy enough.

Given that many restaurateurs grow their own vegetables and that others simply buy what they like the look of in markets, it was hard to find a supplier of the sort that we discovered for the other kinds of produce discussed in this book.

However, a little way out of Quarré les Tombes, in the Morvan, we came to a farm that is also a market garden. Gérard Maternaud is a stocky, middle-aged man with a strikingly young face, a snub nose, bright blue eyes and rich brown, wavy hair. The farm belonged originally to his great-grandparents. Traditionally, they kept a herd of Charolais, but when Gérard took over in 1972, he found that beef was no longer economic.

He decided to diversify and started to grow strawberries, because he found that where he is they come late. The French are very keen on micro-climates. He gets more rain than farmers only 5 km (3 miles) away. The granite soil, very different from that of the beech woods we passed through on the way from Quarré les Tombes, can also make as much as fifteen days' difference in the ripening of his berries; moreover the natural potassium gives them more taste.

From this modest beginning Gérard has built up a thriving concern, becoming both a grower and a wholesaler, dealing in fruit, flowers, vegetables, and even Christmas trees. His greatest pride is the 8 hectares (20 acres) of land on which he grows his vegetables – carrots, lettuce, asparagus, cauliflowers, white beetroot, cabbage and mushrooms.

'The most important thing is to take care of the soil, for it is the land that plays the greatest part in producing fine vegetables. I nurture it in the most organic manner possible.' He uses no chemicals, his fertiliser being manure from his cattle. It is partly to this end, as well as for sentiment, that he still keeps a herd of 42 Charolais. He does not plough up the land; to keep down the weeds he uses the amazing, hissing machine mentioned on page 137.

Everything is geared to quality. 'I could grow twice as much as I do, but not so well. At the same time, one must be practical. I like tiny, young vegetables but cannot produce them in large quantities. They do not keep so well as more mature ones, so it is not economic for anyone, neither the producer nor the customer.'

While Gérard may not be quite so folksy as some of our other suppliers, his standards are of the same calibre. Although he employs eight people, his is still a family business. Apart from supervising the farm and the growing, Gérard goes himself to the market to buy produce for the wholesale side of the enterprise. His father makes the deliveries, 'up to a distance of 70 kilometres [42 miles], though not for just one bag of carrots.' His daughter keeps the accounts.

One needs no more evidence that his produce is of the highest quality than the fact that among his regular customers are two Michelin three-star restaurateurs, Bernard Loiseau at Saulieu and Marc Meneau at St-Père-en-Vézelay.

Velouté d'asperges aux pointes d'asperges

CREAM OF ASPARAGUS SOUP WITH ASPARAGUS TIPS

For 4

2 kg (4¼ lb) green asparagus
3 tablespoons *crème fraîche*
juice of 1 lemon
coarse salt and freshly ground pepper

Peel the asparagus with a peeler from near the tip to the end. Cut off about 2 cm (¾ in) from the hard and fibrous end. Wash the stalks delicately so they don't break, and do so quickly so they don't become bitter.

Bring 3 litres (5¼ pints) water to the boil with 3 tablespoons coarse salt, and cook the asparagus for 7-8 minutes over a high heat. Drain, and refresh in cold water. Drain again and cut the tips off. Reserve these in a warm place.

Blend the stems to obtain a purée, then push through a sieve. Put this purée in a pan, add the *crème fraîche* and lemon juice, and mix. Heat gently, and season with salt and pepper.

Pour the thick soup into warm plates and garnish with the warm asparagus tips. Serve immediately.

Ragoût de légumes

VEGETABLE STEW

For 4

4 large carrots, peeled
4 small turnips, peeled
20 tiny onions, peeled
2 large courgettes, washed and trimmed
200 g (7 oz) French beans, topped and tailed
200 g (7 oz) shelled fresh green peas
100 g (4 oz) butter
2 sprigs of chervil
juice of ½ lemon
salt and pepper

Cut the carrots in four lengthwise, and cut out the hard centre. Cut the strips into 3-cm (1¼-in) long sticks. Cut the turnips into similar strips. Put the carrots, turnips and onions separately into three small pans, add 20 g (¾ oz) butter to each plus a pinch of salt and enough water to just cover. Simmer for 10-15 minutes until tender but still crunchy. Drain well.

Don't peel the courgettes. Cut them in half lengthwise, and remove the seeds. Cut the flesh in strips the same size as the other vegetables. Melt the remaining butter in a frying pan large enough to hold all the courgette pieces in one layer. Place them on the bottom, skin upwards, and brown. Cover with salted water, cook for 2 minutes, then take off the heat. Drain, but reserve the liquid.

Cook the peas and the beans separately in salted water (the peas for 5 minutes; the beans for 8); do not cover, so that they remain green. Drain and cool under cold water. Drain well again.

Cut the leaves from the chervil and keep in a bowl of fresh cold water until needed.

When all the vegetables are cooked, put them together in a big pan with the cooking juices of the courgettes. Heat up slowly, season and add the lemon juice just before serving. Divide the stew between the plates and sprinkle the chervil leaves over each.

Bernard Loiseau

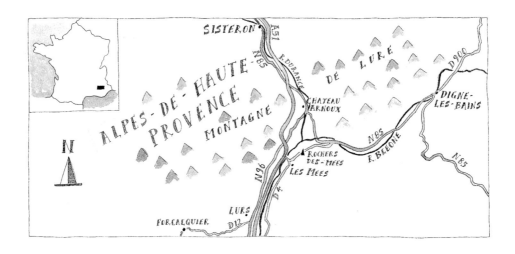

Olive Oil

Not far from Digne, on the left bank of the Durance river, as it flows to join the Rhône at Avignon, there is a curious rock formation, known as Les Mées. What we take to be wind erosion has carved out of the cliff a row of cigar-shaped upright columns, fat in the middle and tapering at the top. In medieval times they thought otherwise. These stones were once some forty monks in their cowls, lapidarised for all time, like Lot's wife, as a punishment for debauching the girls in the village.

On the opposite bank of the river, below the high, romantic monastery of Ganagobie are groves of olives. It is the oil from these olive trees that Pierre and Jany Gleize of La Bonne Etape at Château-Arnoux use in their superb Provençal cooking.

Although France produces only a tiny proportion of the world's olive oil, perhaps 0.1 per cent, as compared with the 75 per cent produced by a combination of Spain, Italy and Greece, there is a wide variation in the kinds of oil made. The lighter oils of Provence come from the *Bouches du Rhône*, notably round Maussane, near Arles, where they pick the olives early when they are still very green, while heavier oils come from further north, most famously from Nyons in the Drôme, where the olives are left until they are black – the only difference between green and black olives being the stage at which they are picked.

Julien Masse produces his olive oil by methods that have not changed for a hundred years or more. His presses date from the last century; many of his tools he has carved himself from the wood of his trees.

The oil from the region of Les Mées is certainly rougher, which is what the Gleizes like, especially for the dish they make with *cèpes* that would kill the taste of a more refined oil.

Their supplier, Julien Masse, is a crotchety old man of at least 70 and as gnarled as his olive trees, some of which, he maintains, are 1,000 years old. This is probably untrue. The Mediterranean olive (*Olivea europea sativa*) is indeed long-lived, but its reputation of near immortality stems from the fact that when an old trunk withers, shoots appear from its base that grow into a new tree.

Young trees will bear no fruit for at least four years, often not for ten. Their period of full maturity and greatest productivity lasts from the age of about 33 years to 150. Olives, like all other fruit trees, have to be pruned, and benefit from a lot of care. Pruning nowadays is done preferably every year, although this is a comparatively recent departure. The Romans, for example, pruned only once every eight years.

'You will recognise my trees,' said M. Masse, 'because I keep them tidy, scything the grass around to let them breathe. The others don't bother. Today no-one works with his arms. All they think about is machines – tractors, aeroplanes and all the rest, what? My fields are cleaner than my house.' And so it proved.

M. Masse's trees stand out from those of his neighbours because he tends the soil round them with the care of a proud housewife.

Julien Masse is a passionate advocate of the benefits of olive oil. He maintains that everyone should consume at least 20 litres (42 pints) a year for good health.

When we went to look at his trees, they stood out from the surrounding olive groves, each one cosseted and cared for, with bare earth around its base.

Masse's thick, nasal accent made him extraordinarily difficult to understand, and he was singularly uncommunicative most of the time, though with unlooked-for bursts of friendliness. His mill lies a few miles from the town of Forcalquier, once the summer seat of the Counts of Provence, one of whom, in the thirteenth century, managed to marry his four daughters off to four kings – France, England (Henry III), the Two Sicilies and the Holy Roman Emperor (Richard of Cornwall).

Such grandeurs are long forgotten and Masse's mill is a modest place, lying below a back road by a bend in the small river. It is a pretty place, popular with young lovers who, in the heat of the summer, come and swim naked in the mill pool and then make love on the banks, little realising that Masse has a hideaway where he sits and watches.

Here he has worked for 55 years. When he started, it was a flour mill and it provided bread for three villages nearby. Now he is concerned only with olive oil, produced strictly *à l'ancienne*, as his labels proudly announce. When he says *ancienne*, he means it. Under the mill house there are two, dark, smoke-blackened rooms. In the further one there is a double mill-wheel, with two vast stones for crushing the olives, driven by a Heath-Robinson arrangement. It is more than 100 years old.

For the whole month of January, Masse, his two nephews and one nephew's wife work in the afternoons, picking the olives. 'She is far stronger than them,' he says crossly. In the morning, they crush the previous day's pick in the mill. They pack the pulp that results into circular fibre envelopes shapes like enormous Breton berets. These are then piled one on the top of the other to a height of 2.5-3 m

Green olives are the ones that are picked early; black olives are matured until the new year.

(8-10 ft) in a press as aged as the mill. The press bears down and the oil pours out into a tank, the first prized 'cold virgin pressing'. Water is put into the tank to drive any sediment down and the oil is drawn off.

Modern methods squeeze out more oil, in particular the centrifuge, of which Masse speaks with fierce contempt, asserting that, in extracting the oil, it also takes out the flavour. Masse is interested only in this first pressing. The detritus of the fibre sacks piles up on the floor, capable in thrifty eyes of producing more oil. These remnants he sells to some Italians.

Masse's oil may be something of an acquired taste, but it is the true oil of Provence, as old-fashioned as its maker. Recent years, up until 1992, have been hard for Masse. Normally he hopes to produce 4 tons of oil, but he had four bad years in a row, counting himself fortunate to make 1½ tons. It takes 5 kg (11 lb) of olives to make a litre (1¾ pints) of oil.

As with all forms of agriculture, nothing ever seems quite right, and nature's whims conspire against the farmer. When the trees are in flower in May, the wind must blow to scatter the pollen. Too dry a summer is bad; there must be some rain and the sun must not shine so cruelly as to shrivel the fruit. The moon, of course, plays its part, but quite what part was hard to follow in Masse's *patois*.

The old man's mildly misanthropic nature unbends a little when he starts to talk of the benefit to health to be had from olive oil. 'Every day with my *soiron* [evening soup] of vegetables, I eat olive oil. Look at me. Everyone should have 20 litres a year for good health, I have surely 24 litres.'

Throughout the ages, people have been extolling the virtues of olive oil. Hippocrates, in the fifth century BC, recommended it for cholera and ulcers; the elder Pliny, 600 years later, advised it for, *inter alia*, headaches, inflamed gums and pustules round the eyes. It is also reputed to relieve high blood pressure, restore hair to balding heads and remove water stains from polished furniture!

Its best purpose remains its use in the cooking of such chefs as Pierre and Jany Gleize.

Salade de cèpes au mesclun

CEPE AND MIXED LETTUCE SALAD

Per person
1 medium *cèpe*
a handful of *mesclun* (as many different kinds of
lettuces as possible), washed and dried
about 2 tablespoons olive oil (from *Les Mées*)
a dash of good wine vinegar
juice of ⅛ lemon
salt and pepper

Choose mushrooms which have been picked
when the weather is dry, so they are not too
wet. Wipe, then slice very finely with a
sharp knife.

Toss the lettuce leaves in a little oil and
vinegar, then make into a small bed on the
plate. Form a spiral dome of *cèpe* slices on the
leaves. Season with lemon juice, salt and
pepper and enough of the remaining olive oil
to cover the *cèpes*.

The olive oil from *Les Mées* is particularly
recommended for this recipe, as, more
than other oils, it complements the taste
of the mushrooms.

Noisettes d'agneau au thym, courgettes et aubergines

LAMB *NOISETTES* WITH THYME,
COURGETTES AND AUBERGINES

Per person
3 lamb *noisettes* (cut from the loin)
100 ml (3½ fl oz) strong lamb stock (see
method)
100 ml (3½ fl oz) olive oil
1 teaspoon fresh chopped thyme
1 small courgette, washed and trimmed
1 baby aubergine, washed and trimmed
salt and pepper

If you buy loin of lamb or lamb chops, keep
the bones and make a strong stock with
them, adding an onion, some carrot, peppercorns and a *bouquet garni* (bay leaf, parsley
etc). Simmer for about 3 hours, then boil to
reduce. Strain.

In a hot frying pan, fry and seal the meat,
seasoned with salt, pepper and thyme, for
minutes only, until pink.

Slice the courgette and aubergine finely,
and fry them separately in the olive oil.

On the plate, arrange the vegetables
nicely, and put the lamb *noisettes* on the top.
Coat with the reduced lamb stock.

Pierre and Jany Gleize

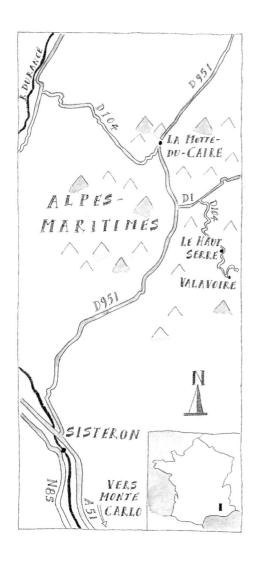

Pigeons

This is not the Provence of popular imagination – not the villa-ridden Riviera coast with its memories of Edwardian gamblers and the 1920s playboys of Scott Fitzgerald, nor the sun-worn farms of Cézanne with their rippling orange roofs, nor even the fancied Provence of the recent *émigrés* from Northern Europe. This is a harsh land, steep with sharp, limestone crags, the forerunners of the true high Alps, whose peaks shine not far away, a startling white in the sky of faultless blue.

Here Claire Dillard breeds possibly the best pigeons to be found in France. It is appropriate that she should live in Provence, because from there came the first moves to break the feudal stranglehold over the breeding of pigeons.

From medieval times, none but the nobles had the right to own a pigeon-house, a dovecote or an aviary. The intention was to protect crops from the ravages of birds. The Provençaux, being of an independent turn of mind paid less and less attention to this law, so that by the end of the seventeenth century, with wider land distribution, *pigeonniers* were springing up everywhere. A general tax was proposed. The new landholders protested to the King. After a ten-year battle, they won, and the right to own a *pigeonnier* was established for all.

Claire Dillard is surprisingly not a Provençale, but a Parisienne. She and her husband, a printer by profession, bought their lonely farmhouse, with its 32 hectares (80 acres) of rocky hillside and its broad mountain views, fifteen years ago.

'We came to find solitude and space. The house was a ruin and it took us five years to restore it, working in our holidays.' When it was finished, Madame Dillard needed something else to do. So she started pigeon breeding as her own particular enterprise. She now has 600 couples of birds. They live in large aviaries not far from the house, which one might think would be aggravating and noisy, disturbing the peace that the Dillards came here to find. 'They are quite peaceful, you know. Happily, 1,000 pigeons make no more noise than one pigeon.'

Claire Dillard makes pigeons sound far more agreeable than one might suppose if one's acquaintance with them were limited to the creatures which infest the pavements and rooftops of most cities.

'They are, of course, monogamous and a couple will live together for quite five years, breeding contentedly. In this way, they are so much better than quails, which have a very short breeding span.'

The most important thing is that the birds should not be crowded. If there are too many together, they fight. Madame Dillard puts no more than twenty couples into one aviary. I had expected to see pigeons all of one kind, but in fact there was a jumble of species, varying in colour from pure white, through many shades of grey to a rich, chocolate brown.

Each race has something to contribute to the ultimate ideal pigeon for eating, the principal considerations being taste, conformation or shape – a good round breast being preferred – and productivity. There are other things that differ from

In the solitude and space of the lower Alps, Claire Dillard raises the best pigeons to be found anywhere in France.

race to race such as the colour of the meat, but they are of less importance.

Curiously, the rich brown birds that I admired have an unexpected usefulness in that they are prone to illness, so that they play the kind of role canaries used to play in coal mines, giving warning of potential danger – in this case of epidemics. Pigeons are vulnerable to various diseases, in particular to worms and parasites and to throat infections. As a firm believer in natural products, Madame Dillard relies on essential oils from the herbs and plants of her rough hillsides as the preventatives of disease for her birds – garlic, thyme, oregano, hyssop and lavender.

Certainly her pigeons look well and we had to believe her when she said that they were happy, leading as normal a life as possible. It is true that they never usually leave their cages. However, while we were there, one bird did somehow get out. Far from flying away into the wild, clear sky, it pestered to be let in again.

The birds' diet is of great importance, Madame Dillard insisting that it should be as natural as possible. She would like to grow her own food for them, but the farm, at more than 900 m (3,000 ft), is too high to grow the maize which is their main feed. With the maize, she mixes wheat, other grains and peas, adding also some of those healthy essential oils.

Each bird is given a number when it hatches and its pedigree is recorded. When

Madame Dillard's pigeons are very tame. They live in spacious cages about 90 m (100 yds) from the old farmhouse which the Dillards have restored.

The pigeons are not of one particular breed, but a complete mixture – their distinction comes from the quality of their feed, mostly maize enriched with oils from the herbs of the hillsides.

they are ten days old, the birds come down from the nest and at that stage they are weighed and their progress is carefully monitored from then on. Pigeons mature very quickly. Within a month of their coming down from the nest they are ready.

Each couple produces some twelve or fourteen young each year which means that Madame Dillard has about 150 birds to sell every week. Her birds are killed by hand at the farm and then plucked. This is a contentious question, because the devisers of EC regulations want to prohibit the private killing of pigeons. They want them to go to officially approved abattoirs where they would be electrocuted or killed by automatic throat-cutters, processing 600 birds an hour.

From a gastronomic point of view, this last would be a disaster. Traditionally, pigeons for the table are either smothered or throttled, as it is essential that they should lose no blood.

The quality of Madame Dillard's pigeons may be judged by the restaurants, her main clients, to which she sells – La Bonne Etape at Château-Arnoux, the Gray Albion in Cannes, an excellent little-known restaurant in Aix, the Bistro Latin, and, above all, Alain Ducasse's Louis XV restaurant in the Hôtel de Paris in Monte Carlo.

It would be wrong to call Alain Ducasse the leader of the new generation of chefs because, unlike the group made famous twenty years before by Paul Bocuse, the new chefs of distinction are not a gang. They are individualists, each, as it were, working his own patch, somewhat in rebellion against the superstar image fostered by Bocuse and his *bande*.

Ducasse, then, is the supreme example of these serious and dedicated young men who have brought a new spirit to the world of French cuisine. His career has been marked by a confident determination. On the day that he finished his training at the hotel school in Bordeaux, he telephoned Michel Guérard, the chef who invented *cuisine minceur*, and asked him for a job, offering to work for no wages. After two years with Guérard, he moved on to learn from Roger Vergé at Mougins, which is where he acquired an interest in Provençal cooking. A year later, in 1978, he moved again to Alain Chapel at Mionnay.

The next two years were the most important of his life. Chapel was unquestionably the greatest chef at the time. He was passionately concerned about the quality of the produce he used, he went to any lengths to cultivate and encourage his suppliers, and he had a great feeling for his region of France. He inspired Ducasse to such an extent that, even today, three years after Chapel's death, Alain puts in with every bill in his restaurant a note urging his customers to visit the restaurant now run by his widow.

When Alain left Mionnay, he worked again for Vergé, running his second restaurant, and then ran the kitchens of the Hotel Juana at Juan-les-Pins, where he gained two Michelin stars.

In 1987, the Société des Bains de Mer, which owns the casino in Monte Carlo and is itself partly owned by Prince Rainier of Monaco, offered Alain the job of Chef des Cuisines at the Hôtel de Paris. With characteristic confidence, Alain made demands that others thought excessive, but the Société knew what it wanted and gave him everything he asked for. He has total command over everything to do with food and drink in the hotel, from room service to banqueting. His kitchens cover an area of more than 1,000 square m (3,300 square ft). In these vast kitchens, there is every known device for cooking – wood-fired spits, pot-bellied smokers, bakery ovens (in which he makes fourteen different kinds of bread), tanks in which he keeps live fish and even microwaves.

Alain's own office, covering about 35 square m (116 square ft) looks more like a security guard's office than a chef's refuge. On half a dozen or more television screens, he can watch every corner of his kitchens. It is not that he is suspicious or untrusting of his staff, rather it is that, as a perfectionist, he wants to see everything that happens and be himself responsible for everything.

He uses modern technology to record everything that goes on in his kitchens. He has, for instance, at least 300 recipes that he has devised since he started in 1987 preserved in his computer. He also keeps records of consumption. He can show that last year the Louis XV restaurant used 178 kg (392 lb) of butter, 806 kg (1775 lb) of fish and shellfish, 400 kg (881 lb) of cheese, 292 kg (643 lb) of veal and 384 kg (846 lb) of poultry.

There are 90 chefs working under him, although the most important to him are the whole team of 31, including the washer-up, that he insisted on bringing with him from the restaurant in the Hotel Juana.

The Louis XV restaurant itself is a florid, gilded affair with a painted ceiling showing an unclothed Venus, carved busts of Louis XV's mistresses, Madame du Barry and Madame de Pompadour, and a whole glitter of mirrors. This overblown decor, belonging to the turn of the century, seems to accord ill with the apparent character of the bearded and bespectacled Alain Ducasse, a man plainly more in tune with the twenty-first century. But then he is a person of many contradictions.

The lavish restaurant of the Hôtel de Paris in Monte Carlo, where Alain Ducasse cooks the pigeon to perfection. His cuisine, unlike the decor, is simple and unostentatious.

It would never occur to one to set this son of a duck farmer from the Lande in anything gilded, yet it was he who thought of the slightly precious notion of having a little stool beside each woman's chair for her to put her handbag on.

Equally out of character with the decor is Alain's food. It is not that it is anything but supremely elegant, but that it makes no concessions to snobbery or fashion. Far from splashing any caviar around, he serves such unexpected dishes as pig's trotters, cod and risotto. In fact, his food quite simply reflects his philosophy that great cooking should stem from the finest ingredients, drawn from the region in which the chef lives and which should, in essence, be extremely simple.

In Monte Carlo, Alain has the advantage of the sea, the marvellous vegetables of Provence and the fine produce of Italy. He mixes the traditions of Provence and of northern Italy, taking the best from both, and with the lightest touch provides a cuisine which is both familiar and traditional, and at the same time completely individual and innovative.

He likes Madame Dillard's pigeons because they have, he says, a rustic taste, something nearer game than, for example, the pigeons from Bresse. He says these are much paler and better for poaching rather than cooking in the rich country style that he enjoys.

Amidst all this perfection, it is comforting to find that Alain is more than human, at times lightheartedly humorous and not without culinary faults. His wife will never allow him near the kitchen at home. She says that he dirties too many dishes and sets a dreadful example for their ten-year-old daughter, Audrey.

Poitrine de pigeonneau de nid avec foie gras de canard grillé

YOUNG PIGEON BREAST WITH GRILLED
DUCK *FOIE GRAS*

For 4

4 young pigeons, about 400 g (14 oz) each in
weight, carefully cleaned
4 thin rashers lean bacon
4 sage leaves
200 ml (7 fl oz) extra virgin olive oil
100 g (4 oz) butter
200 g (7 oz) raw duck *foie gras*, cut in 4 slices
coarse salt and freshly ground black pepper
Potatoes
1 kg (2¼ lb) new potatoes (try to get them
even-sized, about 50 g/2 oz each)
1 sprig each of fresh sage and rosemary
1 bay leaf
1 garlic clove, lightly crushed
Sauce
1 garlic clove, peeled and chopped
25 ml (1 fl oz) sherry vinegar
2 sprigs of parsley, chopped
a bunch of chervil, chopped
5 basil leaves, roughly chopped
a bunch of chives, finely cut

Have ready a barbecue and coals (or preheat
a grill).

The pigeons: Slip half a bacon rasher and half
a sage leaf under the skin of each of the two
breasts of each bird. Work very carefully so
that the skin does not tear. Cut the legs off
and reserve for another dish. Cut the pigeons
in half along the backbone using poultry
shears. Cut the backbones off completely.
Open the pigeons out and flatten them. Keep
the backbones and necks.

The potatoes: Wash the potatoes clean, then
poach in their skins in salted water with the
sage, rosemary, bay leaf and garlic, about 10
minutes depending on size. They should still
be undercooked and firm. Drain carefully.

When cool, cut into 5 mm (¼ in) slices, and
reserve on a plate under clingfilm.

The sauce: Brown the pigeon backbones and
necks in a deep frying pan with 50 g (2 oz) of
the butter, 85 ml (3 fl oz) of the olive oil, and
the garlic for 10 minutes. Just cover with
water, bring to the boil, then simmer to reduce. Skim the broth several times during
this reduction. When the sauce has reduced
to about 60 ml (2¼ fl oz), strain it. Skim the
fat off the top and reserve the sauce.

To cook: Make sure the charcoal is ready (or
that the grill is hot). Preheat the oven to
230°C(450°F) Gas 8.
   Brush the potato slices with some of the
olive oil and grill them over the charcoal.
Place on a plate and put a tiny piece of butter
on each slice.
   Oil and season the pigeons and grill them
over the charcoal for 10 minutes, turning
after 5. Cool until able to be handled, then
take the breasts and wings off the carcasses.
Cut off the end of the wings.
   Bring the sauce to the boil, add 50 ml (2 fl
oz) of the olive oil, the vinegar and herbs (reserve some of the chives). Season to taste.
   Grill the four slices of *foie gras* over the
charcoal on both sides, seconds only.
   Heat the pigeons and the potatoes through
in the preheated oven for 2-3 minutes.

To serve: Sprinkle the potato slices with
coarse salt and some of the reserved chives,
and season with pepper. Arrange in circles
on warm serving plates, and place pigeon
and the *foie gras* over them. Season with salt,
pepper and remaining chives. Pour a little
sauce over and season with pepper again.
Serve very hot.

Morue de Bilbao rôtie et haricots blancs

ROAST SALT COD WITH HARICOT BEAN
STEW

For 4
4 pieces of salt cod, about 165 g (5½ oz) each
50 ml (2 fl oz) olive oil
1 litre (1¾ pints) milk
1 garlic clove, peeled and thinly sliced
Bean stew
300 g (11 oz) fresh shelled haricot beans (or
dried, soaked or canned, drained)
1 *bouquet garni* (bay leaf, thyme, 1 small onion
pierced with a clove)
2 mild Espelette chilli peppers (or 2 small red
sweet peppers)
150 g (5 oz) butter
2 tablespoons finely chopped flat parsley
a pinch of cayenne pepper
100 ml (3½ fl oz) sherry vinegar
50 ml (2 fl oz) old balsamic vinegar
Garnish
4 tablespoons flat parsley leaves
2 garlic cloves, peeled and thinly sliced
peanut oil for deep-frying

The cod: Soak the cod in cold water, skin upwards, for 48 hours. Change the water every 2 hours during the day. Drain the fish well.

The bean stew: Simmer the beans with the *bouquet garni* in water to cover until tender (minutes if they are fresh or canned, at least 2 hours if dried and soaked).

Fry the mild red peppers in a little of the olive oil. Take out of the frying pan, drain, then peel, seed and cut into strips lengthwise.

Drain the beans, leaving a little of the juices, and remove the *bouquet garni.* Add the butter with a little olive oil. At the last minute, gently mix in the strips of pepper, the parsley, cayenne and the vinegars.

To serve: Poach the cod in boiling milk for 4 minutes, then drain well. Sauté the pieces of fish in hot olive oil with the garlic.

Deep-fry the parsley leaves and garnish garlic until crisp, moments only.

Divide the bean stew between four plates. Arrange the pieces of fish on top, skin upwards, and top with the fried parsley and garlic. Serve hot.

Alain Ducasse

Piments d'Espelette, or mild but piquant red chilli peppers, are named after a little village in the hills behind Biarritz. Every October, the village holds a festival when the houses are festooned with a bunting of red peppers hanging up to dry.

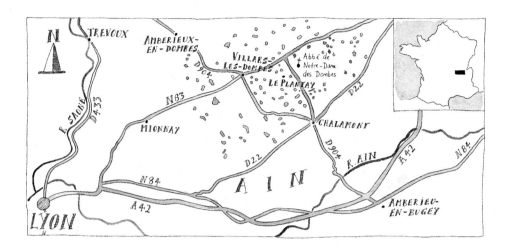

Frogs

La Dombes is one of the strangest parts of France, interesting in all sorts of different ways. It was for centuries a tiny principality that belonged at various times to the Beau, to the Bourbons and to the Orléans. It was much trampled upon, rather in the manner of Belgium, lying as it did between Burgundy and Savoy, both envious of its independence. Its capital, Trévoux, famous in the seventeenth century for its printing press, was in origin a Gallo-Roman town and it was there, until La Dombes was finally brought under the French crown in 1762, that its small parliament sat.

Architecturally the region is attractive, with many Romanesque churches and a large number of fortified houses built of narrow, pink bricks, there being no stone in the area.

No matter from which direction you approach, the land surprises you with the abruptness of its difference from what you have been travelling through – whether it be the vine-covered hills of Beaujolais to the west, the rolling, green pastures of Bresse to the north, or the steep pre-Alps of Bugey to the east. It is a landscape freckled with lakes and ponds, originally a part of the prehistoric Bressane lake that dried up in the primary and secondary geological periods but, as we learned from the court's pronouncements on the area entitled to breed *poulets de Bresse*, belonging itself to the quaternary period rather than the tertiary of Bresse.

The natural propensity for water to gather in lakes was exaggerated in the twelfth century by the development of a system of fish-farming, coupled with

In June, the ponds of La Dombes are covered with lacy sheets of white flowers. By night, the peace of this curious land is fractured by the croaking of frogs.

more ordinary forms of farming. The principle was to have a series of adjoining *étangs* or meres, which were kept as ponds for three years and then each was drained in turn for a year and planted with cereals. The water flow between the ponds was controlled by a primitive kind of valve known as a *thou*. In all, there are at least 1,000 lakes, with a surface area of 10,000 square km (4,000 square miles).

One consequence of all this water has always been an abundance of frogs, and La Dombes is traditionally the source of all the edible frogs of France. When we arrived and saw the colourful expanses of water, surrounded by cushion-clumps of trees and half-covered with a flowering lace of white, we were quite confident that we would find easily lots of *grenouillards* or frog catchers. By day, the ponds were alive with a myriad duck – mallard, pochard, tufted duck, widgeon, shoveller, grebe – and, sure enough, when we wandered out in the damp night air, our ears rang with the scraping croak of frogs.

In the end, the hunt for frog catchers had the quality of a detective story about it. In the first place, no-one could agree as to when the season for catching frogs started. The lady in the *charcuterie* in Villars-les-Dombes said that it began at the end of May and lasted for four months. She would introduce us to her fisherman. She did not know how he caught them, but presumed that it was with a net.

When we went back to ask for the introduction, she said that he had refused to meet us. He caught the frogs in his spare time and did not want anyone asking questions about any affairs that might interest the taxman. It turned out later that the fresh frogs, advertised outside her shop, actually came from the former Yugoslavia.

The owner of the nearby bar was, at first, very forthcoming. He was himself a keen fisherman of frogs. The season, he said, began at the end of June and lasted only a month. When we suggested that he might like to take us on one of his outings, his manner changed entirely. He had little time and, anyhow, it was all different now, as all the *étangs* were privately owned and strictly reserved.

In the restaurant in Bouligneux, near its fine pink-brick castle, we ate some frogs, but the owner said that they came from Albania, flown in alive. His wife was the fishing expert in the family and often went out to catch them, but never for sale in the restaurant. She said that it was illegal to sell frogs caught in La Dombes. They did sometimes have French frogs, from the Jura, which were rather bigger and grey in colour. She thought they were nothing like as good as the smaller, bright green frogs from their own region.

Having faith in the gastronomic leanings of monks, we went to the Abbey of Notre-Dame des Dombes at Le Plantay. The Cistercian Order of Strict Observance founded this abbey in 1863 as part of a programme to relieve the poverty of the area. They introduced many agricultural reforms, but today, while they catch every kind of fish in their broad *étang*, they never catch frogs. Instead of the lively liqueurs one finds for sale at some abbeys, these monks, of whom there are only twenty left, offered only jams and fruit pastilles. Their vow of silence further inhibited any hope of learning much from them. Indeed, we began to despair of ever finding out anything about the famed frogs of La Dombes.

By far the best restaurant in the region is Alain Chapel at Mionnay. Sadly, M. Chapel died in 1990, but his wife carries bravely on and one of his best young pupils, Philippe Jousse, is in charge of the kitchens. Chapel was very concerned always to use whatever the region had to offer. Surely here we would find the genuine article. Philippe was most anxious to help. The only problem was that his local *grenouillard* had just announced his retirement.

Fortunately for us, Philippe was as keen as we were to find a new supplier of true La Dombes frogs. He does cook imported frogs, adding, by the way, that they come not only from Albania and Yugoslavia but also from Greece, Turkey and even Egypt, but says that they are not so good and that he would not, for instance, cook them in butter.

So with Philippe's help, we found ourselves beside one of the pretty meres with René Maisson, a sawyer from Ambérieu-en-Bugey, an engaging character, with a positive obsession about frogs. As he starts to talk about them, his pale blue eyes, under their heavy lids, curiously lacking in eyelashes, sparkle and, despite his

René Maisson has an obsession about frogs. Hooks are forbidden, so he uses a rolled-up piece of nylon stocking as bait. The frog swallows it and is whisked into the frog bag almost before it realises what it has swallowed.

balding head and oddly long ears, he looks more like a youth than a grown man in his middle forties.

'It is a passion. I think about frogs all the time, I even dream about frogs. It is something I have had since I was a child. I haven't the least interest in any other form of fishing. Lately it has been just a hobby. When I was a boy I used to sell them, but that was twenty years ago and now things have changed so much that I just do it for pleasure.'

There is no single thing to which the decline of the La Dombes frog can be attributed. As always, sprays of one sort or another have played a part. There are fewer insects for the frogs to feed off; herbicides have upset the plant life and in some cases made the ponds unhealthy for frogs.

Another important development has been the revival of fish farming, very much on the medieval lines for which so many of the meres were created. As the

Left: *The frogs of La Dombes are smaller, greener and more delicate than those of other regions.* Right: *The summer season sees René out every day wading through the marshy fringes of the* étangs *with his rod and his frog bag.*

barman had said, people now guarded their meres jealously, because much more money can be made by breeding fish in them. The small fry are put into one mere where they spend a year and are then moved into an adjacent mere and so on, leaving the ponds empty in turn for the growing of cereal, usually maize, which flourishes in the rich soil of a drained mere.

La Dombes produces 2,000 tons of coarse fish a year, 60-65 per cent carp which grow to about 1.5 kg (3¼ lb), 20 per cent each of roach and tench, and 5 per cent pike. So it is not surprising that the mere owners do not want people disturbing their waters. It is hard for a frog fisherman to make a living so those that do fish do so part-time and if they do happen to sell some of their catch they want no-one to hear of it.

René says the reduction of the frog population can be judged by the difference in his annual catch. Last year he caught 34 kg (75 lb). As little as two years ago he caught 57 kg (125 lb). Some 3-4 kg (6½-9 lb) in a day means a good day, while he used years ago to expect 10-12 kg (22-26 lb), which is to say between 300 and 350 frogs.

Talking to René was reassuring after all the misleading information we had been given. He was precise about the permitted fishing season, which starts on 29th June and ends at the beginning of October. In winter the frogs sink to the bottom of the meres in order to avoid the ice and there they hibernate. As soon as the sun appears in March, they come to the surface again and mate throughout March and April. By September, the meres are full of young frogs but it is four years before they are big enough to eat.

We learned too that the lady at the *charcuterie* was quite wrong about the method of fishing. The frogs are caught with a rod and line, but it is totally forbidden to use a hook.

'In the old days we used to roll up the skin of a dead frog and attach it to the end of the line. The trick is to wait until the frog has swallowed the bait and then to lift it up quickly and into the bag before the bait slips out of the frog. Nowadays we

use a piece of nylon stocking rolled into a ball. It is a bit rougher and so it does not slip out so easily when one lifts the frog.'

René waded out into the marshy edge of the pond and within moments he gave a deft twist to his rod and a small, emerald frog flew without hesitation straight into his bag. It was, he said, a male. The males are smaller than the females and are in demand for medical research.

As he fished, Philippe talked to him about the culinary aspects. René did not seem as passionate about this side of things. He said he was quite happy to eat them frozen and looked sceptical about the idea that foreign frogs were so inferior in taste. Once they are skinned, he thought, it would be difficult to tell the difference.

Be that as it may, we felt very happy as he continued to pull frogs out of the water. It was plain that Philippe had found his new supplier and that at Alain Chapel, at any rate, one can still hope to eat the true frogs of La Dombes – unless some tedious EC regulation interferes.

Pommes de terre farcies aux truffes blanches, cuisses de grenouilles à la ciboulette

POTATOES STUFFED WITH WHITE TRUFFLES, FROGS' LEGS WITH CHIVES

For 4
1 kg (2 lb) frogs' legs
150 g (5 oz) butter
3 shallots, peeled and chopped
150 ml (5 fl oz) white wine
250 ml (8 fl oz) *crème fraîche*
8 small firm potatoes, scrubbed and boiled in their skins
1 bunch of chives, finely chopped
salt and pepper
Truffle stew
60 g (2¼ oz) white truffles, thinly sliced
1 tablespoon olive oil
1 spring onion, finely sliced
50 ml (2 fl oz) Madeira
250 ml (8 fl oz) *crème fraîche*

Cut and season the frogs' legs. Fry them in about 50 g (2 oz) of the butter in a frying pan. Add the chopped shallots, then pour in the white wine and boil to reduce a little. Take the frogs' legs out of the pan and keep to one side. Add the *crème fraîche* gradually to the sauce, stirring continuously. Let reduce by two-thirds, then sieve.

Bone the frogs' legs and put them back in the sauce, first having taken 2 ladlefuls out. Keep this aside in a small pan. Keep both warm.

Peel the potatoes while still warm, then cut a third off the top to make a 'hat'. Hollow out the remaining two-thirds, leaving a good casing. Fry these casings in 50 g (2 oz) of the remaining butter.

For the truffle stew, heat up the olive oil and fry the spring onion, then the truffles, in it. Simmer gently for a minute, then pour in the Madeira and boil to reduce by two-thirds. Add the *crème fraîche* and let reduce again by half.

In the sauce reserved in the small pan, mix the remaining butter and the chopped chives to obtain a pale green sauce.

Stuff the potatoes with the truffle mixture. Place on plates, top with the hats and pour on a small amount of the green sauce. Arrange the frogs' legs and sauce around the potatoes. Serve immediately.

Gâteau de foies blonds de poulardes de Bresse, sauce aux écrevisses et truffes

CHICKEN LIVER FLAN WITH CRAYFISH AND TRUFFLE SAUCE

For 12

350 g (12 oz) Bresse chicken livers, trimmed
750 ml (1¼ pints) milk
250 g (9 oz) beef marrow
7 whole eggs
7 egg yolks
freshly grated nutmeg and cayenne
salt and pepper
a few chervil leaves
Crayfish and truffle sauce
36 red-clawed crayfish
4 litres (7 pints) fish stock or water
100 g (4 oz) butter
a dash of good brandy (Fine Champagne)
300 ml (10 fl oz) double cream
2 truffles, 50 g (2 oz) each
Hollandaise sauce
2 egg yolks
1 tablespoon lemon juice
100 g (4 oz) clarified butter, melted

Preheat the oven to the very lowest possible heat. Grease a suitable large mould, approximately 17 cm (7 in) in diameter and 7 cm (3 in) deep, with a little extra soft butter, and reserve in the fridge.

Bring the milk to the boil, then season it with salt, a little nutmeg and cayenne. Cool.

In a blender, blend the chicken livers with the beef marrow, the whole eggs and the yolks. Pour the warm milk on to the liver mixture, and blend well. Push through a fine sieve into the buttered mould. Place the mould in a bain-marie and bake in the pre-heated oven for 1-1¼ hours. Check that the flan is perfectly cooked; it should remain soft to the touch.

Meanwhile, boil the garnish crayfish in the fish stock or water for 2-3 minutes, and then shell when they have cooled a little. Melt the butter in a pan and fry the crayfish

flesh for a few minutes. Remove and keep warm. Deglaze the pan with the brandy, add the cream and boil to reduce a little. Slice the truffles and add them to this sauce for a few seconds.

For the hollandaise, make a sabayon by beating together, in a bowl over a pan of hot water, the egg yolks, lemon juice, a tablespoon of water and some seasoning. Then whip in the melted clarified butter.

When the flan is cooked, turn out of the mould on to a serving plate. Surround with the crayfish and truffle sauce, coat with the hollandaise, and decorate with the chervil leaves.

Philippe Jousse

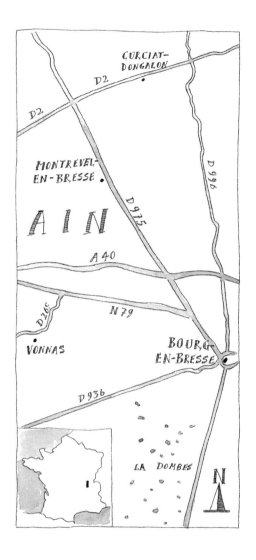

Poulets de Bresse

It is hard to think that a chicken could be an intelligent or a proud creature, yet when one looks at a *Poulet de Bresse*, and especially a fine cockerel, one's contempt is somewhat undermined. With their pure white feathers, great red combs and pale blue feet, they are rather splendid. It may partly be that they are so much healthier than most chickens, but they do, like their owners, seem to comport themselves with an unusual dignity.

Of course, when it comes to eating them, it has been known for centuries that they are the best in the world.

Brillat-Savarin, the great French gastronome, wrote, 'When fattened, the birds of Bresse are to cuisine what canvas is to painters, or the cap of Fortunatus to charlatans. We serve them boiled, roasted, hot or cold, whole or in pieces, with or without a sauce, boned, skinned and every time with the same success.'

It is true that Brillat-Savarin came from the Department of Ain, which has within its boundaries the largest part of the area designated as being entitled to mark its produce as *Volaille de Bresse*, but he had strong support as early as the sixteenth century, when the region belonged to Savoy and the traditional present to the king was a fat capon. In 1601, Bresse was transferred to France and Henri IV spoke highly of the chickens from there.

In 1912, there was even an English society dedicated to promoting the propagation of all breeds of Bresse poultry – President: Lady Wilson, of Addleston, Surrey. Subscription 5 shillings. I can just picture her, with her bustle and her exuberant corsage, prodding at the birds with her frilly umbrella. Alas for British gastronomy, the club had to come to an end in 1936, for that was when things

Gilbert Billoud belongs in the old tradition of breeders of Bresse chickens. Many new EC directives threaten both the quality of the bird and the livelihood of the producer.

became serious and the breeders of Bresse went to law to establish the exact demarcation of their area and the precise rules which govern the breeding of the true *Volaille de Bresse*. La Bresse Club, with its loose talk of 'all varieties' and its pretence that they could be bred in England, had to close.

The court's rulings were detailed and strict. Farmers in neighbouring La Dombes, for instance, had to give up any claim to be producers of Bresse chickens. Geologically speaking, La Bresse belongs to the tertiary period, having virtually no chalk, whereas La Dombes is firmly in the quaternary. The acids that there are in the soil act as a bleach, contributing to the whiteness of the Bresse chicken's feathers and to its blue feet. The lack of chalk, however, means that the birds' skeletons are thinner and lighter, so that a customer buying *Volaille de Bresse* gets more actual meat for her money. The soil and the deposits in it are quite different, so that grits the birds peck at, the herbage that grows on it and the insects that live in it are all different, and this is of grave importance, as we shall see.

In 1957, the Bresse farmers got their *appellation contrôlée*. Cattle and sheep have pedigree herds so that there is no need for other controls. No-one can pretend that a cow is a Charolais or a Limousin; either it is and there is a registered pedigree to say so, or it isn't. It was therefore a great triumph to win this recognition for a chicken. In an area of about 100 by 40 km (60 by 24 miles), there are now some 600 farms producing *Volaille de Bresse*. While it is not a difficult form of farming, the farmers have to be scrupulously careful not to infringe any of the inviolable rules.

The first and most attractive rule is that the birds must live a great part of their lives out-of-doors, in the green pastures of the countryside. They must be put outside at the latest when they are five weeks old and then must stay out for a minimum of nine weeks in the case of ordinary chickens, male or female, twelve for fat hens or *poulardes*, and eighteen for capons. One young producer, Daniel Blanc, told me that he always puts them out at two or three weeks, provided the weather is reasonable, and his often stay out for as much as eighteen weeks, although he does not raise many capons. They do, of course, have to be shut up at night for fear of foxes and, according to Daniel, by day, the crows of the region, working in highly organised groups of three or four, present a real threat to the young chicks.

The regulations state that each bird must have an area of pasture to wander in of at least 10 square m (12 square yds). In the event, nearly all the good farmers allow their birds far more space. Indeed, one of the pleasures of La Bresse is to see the flocks of liberated birds roaming over the fields and into the woods.

The court in 1936 waxed quite lyrical about the life of the young chicken: 'at liberty all day in the meadows, where she finds the animal nourishment of insects, molluscs and worms; where she enjoys a gymnastic wandering, developing her muscles; where the solar radiations pour down on her, her animal nourishment being supplemented by distributions of grain and a cake made mostly of maize.'

The dietary rules are as rigid as the others. At no time may the birds eat anything other than maize, wheat and full or skimmed milk – except for what they grub up in the fields which, from the singular nature of the soil, is unlike what other, and we must believe lesser, chickens find. The milk can be in powdered form and makes up 6–10 per cent of the cake, while the wheat represents 20 per cent, the bulk being maize. Absolutely nothing else may be added – especially no antibiotics, hormones or chemicals to stimulate growth. In fact, with their healthy way of life, Bresse chickens are remarkably free from disease.

Daniel says that controllers come at irregular intervals and take away three birds to check them for any infringement.

He buys day-old chicks from an approved breeder and raises 6,000 birds a year on the 35 hectares (87½ acres) that he works by himself as a mixed farm, although his elder brother, who farms elsewhere, does help him with big tasks. The finishing period of the birds' life, spent in cages, lasts between eight and fifteen days and is the only mildly unpleasant portion of their upbringing. When they are

The rules of the appellation contrôlée *mean freedom and a healthy life for the chickens, each of which must have a minimum of 10 square m (12 square yds) of pasture.*

sent to be killed, the ordinary chickens must be four months old and weigh 1.5 kg (3¼ lb), the fat hens or *poulardes* must be five months and weigh 2.1 kg (4½ lb), and the capons eight months and weigh 3.8 kg (8¼ lb).

Daniel is in his twenties and is unusual in that most of the breeders are in their late fifties. Perhaps more typical of the old ways is the family Billoud. Gilbert Billoud is gloriously proud of the traditions of Bresse, boasting of the many centuries during which it has been famous for its chickens. He used to rent the farm he works, which in his youth was the normal pattern – even with many of the romantic-looking, timber-framed houses with their supplies of maize, also bleached white by the soil, hanging under the broad eaves, which one might have supposed would have been in the same family for generations. Rent had to be paid twice a year, which took a lot of careful saving and economic judgement.

Gilbert was most proud of his capons, possibly because they are so demanding and also so precarious an undertaking. The young males destined for this particular fate are castrated at the age of twelve weeks. The operation is performed under the wings and, Gilbert says, the birds recover quite quickly. He showed us the scars on one of his birds and they were small and plainly not troublesome.

Nonetheless, about half the capons are lost, one way and another, which, coupled with the greater length of time that they have to be kept (from April until December), is what makes them expensive.

Both Daniel and Gilbert, partly because of the complicated modern regulations about the slaughter of animals, sell their finished birds to a wholesaler, Jean-Claude Miéral at Montrevel-en-Bresse, who looks after about 60 of the 600 producers. But even he has trouble with the EC dictates about slaughter. Electrocution, which is the method favoured by the bureaucrats of Brussels, is inclined to break the rather fragile skeletons of the *Volaille de Bresse*, making them unsaleable. Lightness is one of the qualities for which Bresse chickens are admired. In fact, Jean-Claude says, they have in recent years been getting slightly heavier and there is a determined effort on the part of breeders to get back to the old weight. If successful, it will make their bones even more vulnerable to electrocution.

'The EC laws all militate against the producer and are destroying the traditions of good food,' said Jean-Claude. This was a cry that we heard again and again, from the cheese-makers, the pigeon breeder, the *foie gras* makers, and from nearly every restaurateur.

Jean-Claude is as fiercely proud of his Bresse chickens as are his producers, knowing the exact qualities to expect of each bird that he buys and, in the case of restaurants, knowing the dishes that his customer cooks. 'Each chef wants a different bird. It depends, of course on what he is going to do with it.'

When it came to a question of which restaurant to select for the *Volaille de Bresse*, there was really no choice, although I cannot resist mentioning Léa in Montrevel-en-Bresse, where we had one of the most agreeable lunches of our

Outside the Bresse farmhouses, ears of corn hang from the eaves – maize, wheat and skimmed milk being the only food allowed, apart from what the birds peck from the ground. The soil and the insects of the region are believed to contribute much to the quality.

many journeys, the chicken being the success that Brillat-Savarin predicted. But the king of all the chefs in Bresse is Georges Blanc of Vonnas, who is, incidentally, also the President of the Interprofessional Committee of *la volaille de Bresse*.

The Blanc family can trace their origins back through many generations of Bresse farmers, but it was his great-grandparents who moved to Vonnas and became innkeepers. When his grandfather took over the business in 1902, his grandmother became so skilled in the kitchen that Curnonsky, the great gastronome of the 1920s, called her 'the best woman chef in the world'. Georges Blanc's mother kept the spirit of the place alive until, in 1968, Georges took over.

His arrival had the quality of typhoon. By no means gradually, the country town inn, once the meeting place of farmers on their day out at the market, was transformed into a grand restaurant and hotel of the first quality. In 1981, he won his third Michelin star and *Gault-Millau* proclaimed him chef of the year. In the corner of the town where the hotel is, everything seems to belong to Georges Blanc. There is a small *auberge* decorated in the style of 1902, which, by the way, serves the best 120-franc menu I've had in France; there is a building called La Résidence, a row of boutiques, and at least one, if not two wine stores, all blazoned with the name Georges Blanc. There are sundry piazzas and lanes and corners all called after a member of the Blanc family. He even has his own vineyard, producing a perfectly acceptable Chardonnay. In the end, it comes as quite a surprise to go into the Post Office and find that it does not belong to him.

All this commercialism makes one suspicious. It seems to belong to the rather dubious aura created by that inflated self-publicist Paul Bocuse and his *bande*. There is, however, no need to worry. Georges Blanc's restaurant is well worthy of his famous grandmother – La Mère Blanc. Georges is carefully devoted to her example of using local produce and cooking it simply. He is also interested in what might be called the scholarly side of cooking and has a considerable knowledge of the history of food.

The first of his recipes is, naturally, one using Bresse chicken.

Poularde de Bresse à la crème façon grand-mère Blanc

GRANDMOTHER BLANC'S FAT BRESSE HEN IN CREAM

For 6

1 fat hen from Bresse, about 1.8 kg (4 lb) in weight
150 g (5 oz) butter
2-3 tablespoons plain flour
3 egg yolks
500 ml (17 fl oz) double cream (or *crème fraîche*)
a little lemon juice
salt and pepper
Aromatic garnish
1 whole onion, peeled and pierced with a clove
1 garlic clove, peeled
1 sprig of thyme
½ bay leaf

If not already prepared, clean the hen then singe it over a flame to burn off the feather stubs. Keep the giblets. Cut the bird into eight pieces thus: divide both legs into two; cut off the wings and trim the pinions; cut the breasts off the carcass (these will be cut in half after cooking). Reserve the neck and the wing pinions.

In a large lidded casserole or pan, sauté the eight chicken pieces in 120 g (4½ oz) of the butter. Add salt and pepper, and cook until golden brown.

Add the aromatic garnish ingredients, the giblets, the wing pinions and the neck. Add the remaining butter and the flour. Let brown, stirring, then moisten with enough water to cover the meat. Bring to the boil to thicken the sauce, then cover and simmer for about 30 minutes, depending on the size of the chicken pieces.

In a large bowl, beat the egg yolks with the cream and reserve.

When the meat is cooked, transfer it all, using a slotted spoon, to another saucepan. Discard the giblets, neck and wing pinions. Strain the sauce, discarding the aromatic garnish ingredients, and pour it back on to the meat. Over a low heat, pour in the egg and cream mixture, stirring continually and taking care not to let it come to the boil. (If it becomes too thick, add a little water or extra cream.) Check the seasoning, add a dash of lemon juice, and serve immediately on a heated platter, with some rice or potato pancakes.

Poivrons farcis

STUFFED RED PEPPERS

For 4
4 red peppers
Stuffing
100 g (4 oz) short-grain rice
1 onion, peeled
50 g (2 oz) button mushrooms
1 small courgette, trimmed
1 small aubergine, trimmed
1 cooked artichoke heart
1 tomato, skinned and seeded
½ green pepper, seeded
150 ml (5 fl oz) olive oil
1 hard-boiled egg
50 g (2 oz) green peas, boiled in salted water
1 fresh egg
50 g (2 oz) Gruyère cheese, grated
a pinch of grated Parmesan cheese
salt, pepper and paprika
To cook
1 onion, peeled
4 garlic cloves, peeled
4 sprigs of thyme
2 bay leaves
50 ml (2 fl oz) olive oil
To serve
50 g (2 oz) unsalted butter
paprika or similar spice
50 g (2 oz) green peas, boiled in salted water

The peppers: Clean the peppers and cut off the tops, keeping them to make 'caps'. Seed the peppers carefully and keep to one side.

The stuffing: Boil the rice in salted water in a covered pan until cooked. Cool under cold water and drain well. Put in a bowl.

Cut into fine cubes the onion, mushrooms, courgette and aubergine (both un-peeled), artichoke, tomato and green pepper. Fry all these ingredients in the olive oil until just softened, then add seasonings to taste. Drain and add to the rice in the bowl. Chop the hard-boiled egg finely and add, with the peas.

Beat the fresh egg with the Gruyère and Parmesan cheeses, then add to the stuffing and mix well. Fill up the red peppers, pushing the stuffing well down inside, and cover them with the 'caps'.

To cook: Preheat the oven to 180°C(350°F) Gas 4.

Finely chop the onion and crush the garlic and make a bed of these in a greased oven-proof dish large enough to hold the peppers. Set the peppers upright on this bed. Add some salt and pepper plus the thyme and bay leaf, and moisten with the oil. Cook in the preheated oven for 40 minutes. Remove and cool for about 10 minutes.

To serve: Cut the red peppers into slices, about 3 cm (1½ in) thick. Serve with the butter heated lightly and beaten with a little water to make an emulsion, seasoned with paprika, and with the warm green peas.

Georges Blanc

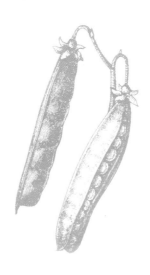

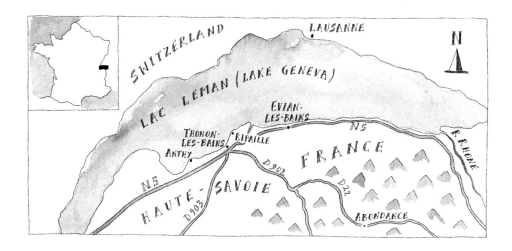

Char

When the clouds hang low over Lac Léman and the water lies as still as gunmetal, there is, down by the shore, a prehistoric quiet, so that it is easy to imagine a mammoth looming out of the mists. And so, 10,000 years ago or more, one did, and lost its tusk near Thonon-les-Bains.

We know little more of the place until the fifth century, when the region was settled by the Burgondes, a rough Germanic people from the Baltic, who were known for eating a lot of onions and garlic. They were additionally smelly because, like the Tibetans and the Oromo tribe in Ethiopia, they greased their hair with rancid butter. They were the ancestors of the Burgundians.

Squabbled over, more than fought over, this area wavered to and fro in both temporal and spiritual matters. The secular choice lay between what ultimately became Burgundy and the Humbertian Italian kingdom of Savoy, which predominated from the eleventh century. It was finally annexed by Napoleon III as a part of France in 1860. The religious choice was between the Roman Catholics and the Protestants, until St Francis de Salis, by his lively preaching, won the area ultimately for Rome at the end of the sixteenth century, undoing all the work of the Calvinist, Guillaume Farel, whose success some half century before had caused much agitation.

I thought of the mammoth one damp morning when waiting by the lakeside for Pierre Portier, the fisherman, and John Brunton to come back for breakfast. Pierre's cabin sits on the shore a few kilometres west of Thonon. It consists of two

Pierre Portier is one of the last 50 fishermen left on the French side of Lake Geneva. The numbers have halved in the last 30 years. Overleaf: It is a hard life. M. Portier gets up most mornings at 3 a.m. to set off with his nets.

rooms, one of which holds a huge refrigerator. In the other there is a bed because, although he has a house where he and his family live, he goes fishing every day at three o'clock a.m. It was a morning of still beauty and it seemed a perfect day for mammoths.

The only thing to loom out of the mist was Pierre's boat, the bottom of it wriggling with the fish he had gathered from his nets – a lot of perch, a fair number of roach, some white fish and rather few *ombles-chevaliers*, the most prized fish of Lac Léman, as those on the French shore call Lake Geneva.

It was barely nine o'clock but Pierre settled us down beside his hut with a huge loaf of bread, some Abondance cheese and a fine bottle of wine from the Château de Ripaille, the elaborate, fifteenth-century castle of the Counts of Savoy a few miles to the east.

Pierre is a naturally happy man, with a round, red face, luminous green eyes and the rich voice of a singer. He has a passionate interest in good food and when he was nineteen started a restaurant, but it failed for his lack of experience.

'I rent this plot from the *commune*. If I owned it, I would have a restaurant here and cook what I catch.'

Pierre is one of a dwindling band of fishermen. 'In 1960 there were 300 of us on the lake. Now there are 110 on the Swiss side and only 50 on the French side.'

Those who live by the lake are very different from the people who live even a mile inland, still affected by the divisions of four centuries ago. 'They are very Catholic, you know, and superstitious, while we are more Protestant. You would not believe it, but in the villages towards the mountains they are terrified of thunder. When there is a bad storm in the night, they get up and pack all their

clothes into suitcases and sit waiting to leave at a moment's notice.'

One cannot imagine what such people make of Pierre's life, for the lake can be quite treacherous, whipping itself into a fury in sudden storms that sweep down from the mountains.

If the life of the fishermen has changed, so has the life of the fish. 'Twenty years ago we started campaigning about the pollution of the lake. The two chief sources are the chemicals that drain off the land from the farms and the effluent from all those factories in Switzerland.

'The fish population has changed significantly. The roach, for instance, are very tough and they have increased lately. The *ombles-chevaliers* are much more sensitive and their numbers have dropped seriously.'

The *omble-chevalier (Salvelinus alpinus)* is known in English as the char or Arctic char. It is a rare fish belonging to the salmon family, found in fresh Arctic waters and in high-lying lakes in northern Europe. They are fairly plentiful, for example, in the Lake District. Oddly enough, in France they are generally associated with Lake Annecy, although they were artificially introduced there as late as 1890, where in good Darwinian style they have developed into a slightly different breed.

They can grow to a maximum of about 75 cm (2 ft, 6 in) long and weigh up to 8 kg (18 lb). They spawn from mid-November to mid-January, laying their eggs (rather more than a trout) on the gravelly bottom of the lake. The young eat plankton and aquatic larva and graduate to little molluscs and small fish. The adults live out in the middle of the lake at a far deeper level than the trout, which live near the surface.

For this reason Pierre's nets for *ombles-chevaliers* are 4 m (4½ yds) wide, with 32 mm (1¼ in) mesh, as opposed to those for perch which are half the width, with a smaller mesh. He has even wider ones, about 20 m (22 yds) wide for catching *féra* (differing authorities translate this as white fish in English, lake herring in American), which live even deeper. His nets are mostly 100 m (110 yds) long.

This matter of nets is another example of change. 'I have 5 km [3 miles] of nets, but in the old days many of the fishermen only had two nets in all.'

Pierre has no use for rods, dismissing them as being all right for children. He is agreeably liberal, though, in his views about amateur fishermen, even if sometimes they disturb the fish.

'We don't own the lake. It is, after all, 86 km [51½ miles] long and everyone has a right to it. Aquatic sports, wind-surfing and water-skiing and speed boats do present a problem, because they are inclined to get entangled in our nets, but they are as much entitled to enjoy their leisure on the lake as we are entitled to earn our living from it.'

Pierre opened another bottle of wine and told us how happy he was. The living he earned from the lake was not luxurious, but it was the life he wanted, even if it seemed to me a hard one. 'If one likes the work, one does not count the hours.'

The char is a comparatively rare freshwater fish, belonging to the salmon family, and is found in high-lying lakes in northern Europe. They live at a deep level, unlike trout, so that the fishermen need wide nets.

The only thing he might regret is the cooking. He has complete confidence, however, in the way that his most valued customer, Charles Plumex, cooks the fish he catches for him, in the best restaurant in Thonon-les-Bains, Le Prieuré.

Plumex is a fine-looking man, his beard and thick hair tinged with red; one cannot doubt that he is descended from those Norse Burgondes, who took over the land fifteen centuries ago. His restaurant, in part of an ancient priory, is of exceptional quality, because Plumex is one of the new generation of chefs who want to break out of the homogeneous pattern created by the chefs of the 1970s and 1980s and to return to more individual and more regional cooking.

All chefs, asked what they like cooking best, say fish, for there is so much more opportunity to create something new, or to express their own tastes than with, say, meat. Charles is therefore lucky to have as his most regional product the fish of Lac Léman, lucky too to have the glorious cheeses of the Haute-Savoie.

A most cultivated man, he is also interested in the history of the region. When he found that the old spice route to northern Europe passed this way, he began to incorporate many spices, such as cardamom, cumin and cinnamon into his dishes.

The char is a more delicate fish than a trout, and therefore needs to be cooked simply rather than with a rich sauce.

The results are as delicious as they are unexpected.

The taste of the *omble-chevalier* is very delicate and for this reason Charles recommends that one does not use too lively a sauce with it. He prefers a little veal stock and some lemon juice. Alternatively he roasts it, using the *beurre de cuisson* or cooking juices. You can poach it, but it will probably taste of the lake. Charles does them with yellow wine from the Jura, reduced with butter and coriander. The locals, he says, often do them in the oven with tomatoes, onions and butter, and are given to overcooking them.

As the chances of most readers' getting hold of either of these fish, unless they live in the north of Britain, are slim, Charles Plumex has given me one recipe for char that can perfectly well be used for trout, and another wonderfully good Savoyard way of doing potatoes. This used to be a dish that the workers ate when they came in from the fields, but is now more commonly used as an accompaniment for game or red meat.

Omble-chevalier au vin jaune et à la coriandre

CHAR IN A YELLOW WINE SAUCE WITH
CORIANDER

For 4

4 char (or trout), about 250-300 g (9-10 oz) each
in weight, cleaned
30 g (1¼ oz) unsalted butter
200 ml (7 fl oz) *Vin Jaune* (yellow wine)
200 ml (7 fl oz) stock (preferably veal)
about 2 tablespoons chopped coriander leaves
salt and pepper

Salt the inside of the fish. Melt the butter in a
hot frying pan, then sauté the fish for about 3
minutes on each side. The fish must be
golden, but take care not to overcook them
or the flesh will lose its tenderness. Do not
burn the butter either. Baste the fish with the
butter whilst cooking. Put the char (or trout)
in a warm place, and keep the butter and
juices.

Place the wine in a small pan, and boil to
reduce by a quarter. Add the stock, reduce a
little more, then add half the cooking juices.
Just before serving, sprinkle in the freshly
chopped coriander.

Coat the fish with the sauce and serve hot.

Farcement de Bernex à la façon de Haute-Savoie

SAVOYARD POTATO AND DRIED FRUIT
GRATIN

For 4

750 g (1½ lb) dried prunes
200 g (7 oz) dried pears
750 g (1½ lb) potatoes
450 g (1 lb) *lardons* (small strips of bacon or
pork belly)
1 tablespoon plain flour
1 egg
50 ml (2 fl oz) Kirsch
a pinch of caster sugar
25 thin bacon rashers
salt and pepper

Soak all the dried fruit in cold water for 24
hours to plump them up. Drain and dry. Pit
the prunes.

Peel the potatoes, then grate them into a
bowl. Fry the *lardons* until golden in a dry
frying pan, then drain and add them to the
potatoes. Mix in all the other ingredients
with the exception of the bacon rashers.

Preheat the oven to 160°C(325°F) Gas 3.

Arrange the bacon rashers round the inside of a large greased dish, then spoon in the
potato mixture. Bake in the preheated oven
in a hot bain-marie for 4 hours.

Charles Plumex

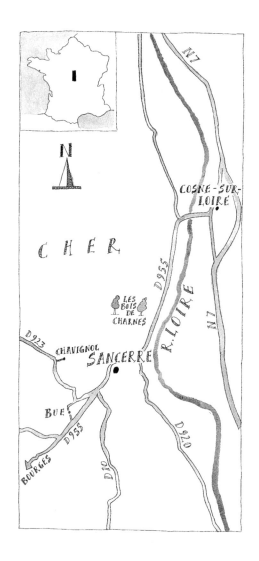

Sancerre

Sancerre is somehow not like other French towns. Seen from the banks of the Loire far below, it looks normal enough, a little like Avalon, perhaps, or Autun, perched on its hill, surrounded by ramparts, its tower and tall roofs spiking the skyline.

Yet, when one has climbed to it, all resemblance to other towns melts away. There is none of the grandeur of Autun nor the openness of Avalon. There is something secretive about Sancerre, with its precipitous, narrow streets and confusing geography. It is hard to find one's way around, although the town is not big. The central square, the Place de la Halle, does not feel like the heart of a community, more like a space that no-one bothered to fill.

Gradually, one becomes aware that everywhere is on two or more levels, that rambling cellars run below many of the houses, so that the entrance to a place may be as much as two streets away from another way out of it.

And, after a day or two, one comes to realise that much of the life of the town is lived also at different levels, riddled with feuds and jealousies, family disputes and bizarre rivalries.

One thing, however, is certain. The whole existence of the town is centred on wine, and this singleness of purpose has always been so, even if the Sancerre wine that insecure diners nowadays order 'to be on the safe side' is, as we shall see, a comparative newcomer.

From several vantage points in the town, one can see the land spreading out, every hillside covered in vines, amounting to a total of 1,500 hectares (3,750 acres) of vineyards. In 582 AD Gregory of Tours made reference to the wines of Sancerre. In the fourteenth and fifteenth centuries, the wines of the region were rated very highly and were produced in such abundance that, in the middle of the sixteenth century, Charles IX ordained that two-thirds of the vineyards should be dug up and the land turned over to cereals and other crops.

No-one paid much attention. During the religious wars, the fiercely Protestant Sancerre was besieged, in 1573, by royalist forces for six grim months. Some 500 of its inhabitants died of starvation; one *vigneron* and his wife were respectively burnt alive and strangled for having eaten the flesh of their little daughter who had died of hunger. The only thing of which the populace never ran short was wine.

The restrictions on production continued for centuries and, even today, for rather different reasons, no grower is allowed to plant more than half a hectare (1¼ acres) of new vines each year.

The most savage restriction of all came in 1886, in the shape of phylloxera. All the vines had to be ripped out and many producers gave up, selling their family holdings. Those that remained set about re-establishing their land in a far better manner than before. During the nineteenth century nearly all the wine produced

The town of Sancerre piles up on a steep hill. From its ramparts, one can see the rich vineyards stretching away for several miles, for the appellation *includes several small villages as well as the main town.*

Twice a year the wine-growers' associations hold a fête du vin, at which new members are initiated. Guests are invited from other associations outside Sancerre and as well as the various initiation ceremonies they attend a solemn mass.

was red, but after phylloxera, the growers made a dramatic decision; they planted almost exclusively the Sauvignon Blanc grape and only a very little Pinot Noir. They set about improving their methods of vinification and no longer shipped off much of their production by river and canal to Champagne to be treated.

The result of this burst of energy was an excellent white wine. By 1936, the growers had achieved the distinction of an *appellation d'origine contrôlée*. This applied only to white wine, but, in 1959, was extended to include Sancerre *rouge* and Sancerre *rosé*. Recently, Sancerre has been enjoying a boom as a fashionable, middle-class wine, being cheaper than Chablis, Meursault, Corton–Charlemagne or other more famous wines. Sancerre is probably appreciated more abroad than in France, and at least half of the production goes for export.

Owing to the relative homogeneity of the soil over a wide area, the wine varies much less from one vineyard to another than in, say, Burgundy. What does make a considerable difference is the method of vinification and here one has a choice between extreme modernity and the highly traditional.

The name Mellot appears over several shops and the entrance to at least two cellars. There is Joseph Mellot and his nephew Alphonse Mellot, but it is as well to know which one you want, because there is a *froideur* between uncle and nephew, one of the many family disagreements in the town.

Alphonse is an exuberant, restless man in his early forties. He has an attractive manner, with an easy smile, his eyes taking in everything that is going on. He talks volubly and is given to much gesture, so that one notices that the tip of the index finger of his right hand is missing. At first, one might take him for something of a playboy, with his Porsche car and his happy, drinking ways. But it soon becomes apparent that he is hard-working, knowledgeable and a sound businessman. Indeed, he is well on the way to becoming the largest producer in Sancerre, which, as well as the Porsche, might be an annoyance to his more sedate uncle.

Going through Alphonse's cellars, one is impressed by the gleaming metal vats, the size of the operation and his mastery of every detail. Alphonse is also an adventurous character. In one bin, there were a few strangely-shaped, blue bottles. These turned out to be an experiment. He had left some vines unpicked until very late, in what is known as a *vendange tardive*, so that the grapes become over-ripe and very sweet. He then made, entirely for his own consumption, a small amount of sweet dessert wine, in the manner of Sauternes, and designed a bottle to put it in. However irregular and unexpected, I thought it rather good, less cloying than many.

No matter how good Alphonse's wine may be, and it is good, we were really looking for a more traditional producer. We talked to several other *vignerons*. They were jolly and hospitable and, by the way, two of them were missing the tips of their index fingers.

In the end there was no doubt that the perfect man was Francis Cottat, whose Sancerre is the only one on the wine list of the Tour d'Argent in Paris. His cellars are not in the town of Sancerre, but in Chavignol, one of twelve or thirteen villages associated with Sancerre and included in the area of the *appellation contrôlée*. Chavignol is famous in its own right for the little goat cheese known as *crottin de Chavignol*, a *crottin* originally being a little earthenware oil lamp in the shape of

On the left is Alphonse Mellot, whose family have been viticulteurs *at Sancerre since 1513; one of his family was wine* conseilleur *to Louis XIV. On the right is Francis Cottat, who was named best wine producer of the Loire valley by* Gault-Millau *in 1992.*

The wine harvest at Sancerre takes place later than in many other wine regions. Alphonse Mellot has even experimented with a tardive, *a late picking, to make a sweet dessert wine.*

which the cheeses are made (although there is a coarser meaning to the word). Since 1976 the cheese has been entitled to an *appellation contrôlée* of its own.

There is nothing old-fashioned about Francis Cottat's appearance. He is a well-preserved man of 63, with pale ginger hair and a face that creases readily with humour. His clothes are not those of the farmer of standard imagination but perfectly up-to-date, even to the point of wearing track shoes.

Many of the *vignerons* used to keep goats as well as make wine, and cheese-making was an equally important part of their livelihood. Since the boom in Sancerre this has become unnecessary, but Francis Cottat kept three goats more out of sentiment than anything. He called them Gina Lollobrigida, Brigitte Bardot and Martine Carol. Unfortunately, Martine Carol was strangled by her rope. In such ways he can appear quite frivolous.

His methods of growing and wine-making, on the other hand, are very austere. In the fields, he does not even use a tractor and quite certainly pours no chemicals on to his land. In almost every respect he differs from the usually accepted modern methods. He harvests his grapes later than most people, and he crushes his grapes with only a hand press. There is no question of metal vats. He matures his wine in old port barrels, some of them 150 years old.

The wine stays in these ancient oak casks for seven to eight months. The question of exactly how long rests with the moon. When the moon is right he will bottle the wine, in a good year filling 30,000 bottles. 'It is the moon that breathes life into the wine.' Cottat is not a superstitious man. It is more that he works by instinct and, in common with so many of our other producers, the moon has a marked influence on his way of thinking. I noticed, moreover, that both his index fingers were intact.

I had become intrigued by this question of index fingers, about which everyone was very reticent. The first time I asked Alphonse about his finger, he dismissed the question, muttering about some accident. It was a friendly wine-waiter, not a native of Sancerre and who happened to be a reader of my books, who suggested the line to follow. 'You will never find out, but you do realise that Bué is the centre of witchcraft in France.'

Bué is one of the villages within the *appellation contrôlée* of Sancerre. It makes no secret of its old connection with witchcraft and the members of its wine-growers' association dress up on festival days as witches or warlocks, with capes and pointed hats. On the surface, it is all a jolly jape, but I cannot help feeling that there is more to it than that.

One evening with Alphonse, when we were all drinking and in a merry frame of mind, he said that he was a member of the Bué wine-growers' association. I asked if he was a witch. He laughed and waggled his truncated finger in my face. 'Of course, what do you think this is?' But he would not speak of it again.

In the Grotte de Lascaux in Périgord, there are many prehistoric paintings of animals, often signed with the palm of a hand. It is thought that the paintings were done before a hunt and depicted the game the hunter hoped to kill. Several of the palm-print signatures lack the tip of the index finger. The probability is that the cave-dwellers cut off the end of their fingers as a kind of sacrifice to ensure success in the chase. Can it be that the *vignerons*, looking for a good harvest, use the same device?

Sancerre is a close-knit place and Daniel Fournier, the chef-patron of the best restaurant in the town, is himself the son of a local *vigneron*. His father had only 5 hectares (12½ acres) and two sons. 'My father told me to find another profession, because there would not be enough to keep us all. Now he has more land and, in some ways, I regret it, but I was always fascinated by cooking since the age of thirteen.'

After leaving hotel school, Daniel worked all over France and then came home to Sancerre. The Restaurant de la Tour is rather an odd mixture, having on the ground floor a seventeenth-century room overlooking the Place de la Halle, and upstairs a modern room with a huge picture-window, giving long views over the vine-covered hillsides. The food, however, is uniformly excellent.

Daniel, like all chefs of his generation, is concerned to use the produce of his region, and naturally uses Sancerre wine in the cooking of his dishes. 'It has an acidity that is good for cooking fish, yet it also has a softness and roundness that it gets from the oak casks in which it is matured, which is useful for white meat.'

Daniel gets salmon and zander (a species of pike-perch) from the Loire, though he fears for them as the damming of the river has lowered the level and water ski-ing pollutes the water. He speaks well of the chickens from the local farms.

The one thing that did give him trouble was his wine-list. He is married to the daughter of another *vigneron* and his brother is married to her sister. He was inclined to promote the family wines. This caused much jealousy. So now he stocks everybody's wine. He does notice, though that, when the *vignerons* come in with a client they order their own wine. If they come in on their own they order a Pouilly or a Bordeaux.

Sancerre is a tricky place, but one I shall always remember with interest.

The vineyards of Sancerre were once given over to red-wine vines. In the replanting which took place after phylloxera struck in the nineteenth century, however, it was almost exclusively the Sauvignon Blanc grape variety which was chosen.

Oeufs pochés au Sancerre rouge

POACHED EGGS IN RED SANCERRE SAUCE

For 4
8 eggs
750 ml (1¼ pints) Sancerre *rouge*
150 g (5 oz) *lardons* (see page 123), finely
chopped
150 g (5 oz) white mushrooms, wiped and sliced
200 g (7 oz) butter
4 shallots, peeled and chopped
250 ml (8 fl oz) stock (preferably veal)
4 slices white bread
4 sprigs of chervil
salt and pepper

For the sauce, fry the *lardons* and mushrooms in 50 g (2 oz) of the butter until the latter have softened. Keep to one side. Fry the shallots in the same pan, adding a little more butter. When soft, pour in the red wine and simmer to reduce the sauce by one-third. Add the stock, and simmer to reduce to 250 ml (8 fl oz) sauce. Add the lardons and the mushrooms to heat through, then beat in half the remaining butter until the sauce is smooth. Season to taste.

Fry the slices of bread in the remaining butter. Poach the eggs. Drain both well on absorbent paper.

On the plate, put two eggs on each bread *croûton*, and coat with the warm sauce. Decorate each plate with a sprig of chervil.

Coq fermier au Sancerre blanc

CHICKEN IN WHITE SANCERRE SAUCE

For 8
1 large free-range chicken, at least 2.25 kg (5 lb)
in weight
1 litre (1¾ pints) Sancerre *blanc*
550 g (1¼ lb) carrots, peeled
2 leeks, trimmed
a sprig of thyme
2 bay leaves
200 g (7 oz) butter
100 ml (3½ fl oz) olive oil
40 g (1½ oz) plain flour
500 g (18 oz) potatoes, peeled
500 g (18 oz) button mushrooms, wiped and
sliced
salt and pepper

Cut the chicken into ten pieces: cut the wings and legs off, and cut the legs into thigh and drumstick. Remove the breasts and ribcage from the lower carcass. Divide each breast in two. Chill until needed.

Make a broth with the chopped lower carcass, 200 g (7 oz) of the carrots, the leeks, thyme, bay leaves and 1.5 litres (2½ pints) water. Simmer for 3 hours.

In a large casserole, brown the chicken pieces in the butter and oil. Pour off most of the fat (keep it), then add the flour to the casserole. Stir well, then pour in the wine and the chicken broth. Bring to the boil, then simmer for 1½ hours, or until the meat is tender.

About 30 minutes before the end of cooking time, add the remaining carrots and the potatoes, both chopped roughly. Sauté the mushrooms in the reserved butter and oil in a frying pan until cooked. Add them to the casserole just before it is ready. The sauce must be smooth.

Daniel Fournier

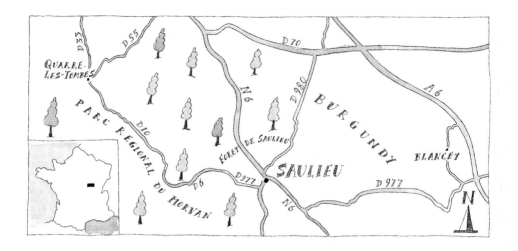

Snails

There is nothing exclusively Burgundian about the snail known as the Burgundy snail. They are the large ones with the striped shell that you can see anywhere in Europe. They are plentiful in the Mendip hills, for instance, though I like to believe that they were imported there by the Romans, who made valiant efforts to improve the standard of Anglo-Saxon cooking.

It is also a myth that snails are a speciality in Burgundy because they fatten up best on vine leaves, although it is arguable that snails can help wine growers in that they only eat the leaves of vines, never the grapes, so exposing the fruit to the sun. It may once have had an element of truth about it, but modern methods of farming have so diminished the number of snails that only about 2 per cent of the snails eaten in France are gathered naturally. The vast majority are imported from eastern Europe and Turkey.

Strangely, in the dark cellars of the Hôtel de Ville of the little town of Sombernon there is an attempt to breed Burgundy snails 'in a scientific manner'. It does not seem to be a very lively enterprise and we have never managed to coincide with whoever runs it in what appear to be fits and starts.

Not far away, the castle at Blancey, just like a score of others in Auxois, sits at the bottom of a steep valley, huddled round with a small village. There is nothing particularly distinguished about it as a building and it has a crumbling air. In front of its main façade, dated 1584, are farm buildings, with a modest house attached to the end of one of them, and it was here that we found a serious raiser of snails.

Jean-François Vadot looked around for a different product to raise on his ancestral beef farm. He settled eventually on snails.

Jean-François Vadot was born and brought up in the castle, but his parents found it impossible to keep up. Since then it has passed through several hands, but he and his family still live in the small house in the farmyard. When they sold the castle, his parents kept about 110 hectares (275 acres) of land on which Jean-François runs a herd of Charolais. There is, however, as we shall see elsewhere, a dwindling demand for Charolais, especially among the better quality restaurants, who want a piece of meat that tastes of something rather than a flaccid lump that can be cut with a fruit knife.

With his high, domed forehead, floating, wispy hair and large, surprised-looking hazel eyes, he reminded me of a nineteenth-century romantic, perhaps Joseph Severn or the young Wordsworth. His ideas are certainly romantic. Wearied by what he called the *banalité* of Charolais, he cast around for something else to breed, preferably something that would bring some general ecological benefit as well as earning a little money. He thought first of breeding ladybirds and selling them to farmers in large numbers, so that the pretty creatures would eat up all the aphids and other annoying bugs and thus free the farmers from the need to use insecticides. He was a little vague as to why he abandoned this project.

His next idea was ostriches. They thrive on quite spare grassland in Africa and could be expected to do well in the lusher pastures of Burgundy. He was convinced of a brisk demand for plumes, which would sell at 100 francs a feather. Then there was the meat. It should be easy to persuade people that the meat was good, and think of the amount of meat on an ostrich leg. Moreover, a very large omelette would need only one egg. He could see endless possibilities.

Again it was not quite clear what deflected him, but he diverted his attention to bison, the ancestor, after all, of all our domestic cattle, and Jean-François is very keen on the purity of race – another reason why he deplores the decline of Charolais which have been debased, in his view, by cross-breeding. He assured me that bison meat is particularly good smoked. In the end he settled for snails.

The snails that he raises are, as it happens, not the Burgundy snail (*Helix* pomatia linne), which does not do well in the artificial conditions necessary for any commercial enterprise. Jean-François raises Gros Gris (*Helix aspersa maxima*), a distinct breed that came originally from Algeria.

He does not actually breed them, this being a difficult business. The sex-life of a snail is complex and somewhat awkward to regulate, as some of it depends on the whim of the snail.

'When one meets a snail, one should always say, "Bonjour Monsieur", never "Bonjour Madame"', says Jean François, 'because all snails are male, except for the brief period when they are actually laying their eggs.'

Snails have a form of penis, just below one eye, which emerges when needed. To mate, two snails link these organs together in an erotic encounter that lasts for eight to ten hours. During this time they exchange semen, each storing the other's in a special reservoir. Thus impregnated, they wander about for an indefinite period looking for a suitable place to lay their eggs. They are extremely fussy, preferring a place that is neither too hot nor too cold, certainly out of the direct sun, often under the leaves of plants, so it may be a matter of weeks before they

For a certain period in warm weather, when they are not tempted to go to sleep, the snails live out of doors in a more natural environment.

As they develop, the snails are kept in groups of the same age and size which overcomes their tendency to cannibalism.

find the right situation. They can lay several hundred. On one occasion a snail laid 2,000, but died immediately. There is a further oddity in that a snail which has laid some eggs may, without any further contact with another snail, lay another batch.

It was in about 1985 that Jean-François and four others decided to form a small co-operative to breed and market snails. It was, as it happened, a good moment as there had been an upheaval in the snail market. A very large number of snails used to be produced in and around Chernobyl. Two days after the nuclear accident, the Greeks bought up the whole stock of snails of the two largest producers in the East, whether contaminated or not, and sold them in the West. This was not quite so cynical as it sounds, because one of the great attractions to a breeder is that it is virtually impossible to have a bad snail. If a snail is alive it is well. As Jean-François puts it, 'a sick snail is a dead snail'.

The five friends agreed that only one of them would do the more demanding task of actually breeding the snails and drew a short straw to see which of them it should be. Fortunately it was not Jean-François.

So he buys eggs from the breeder, who sends them frozen by post, when they have just hatched. A snail's egg is roughly the size of the head of those coloured pins people stick in maps. Its colour is exactly that of a snail's shell which is indeed what it becomes. When it is ready, the baby snail breaks out of its shell in the same way that a bird or a reptile does. The difference is that a snail keeps the greater part of its shell, which then grows with it, for all of its life.

The first month of their life is spent in what Jean-François calls the nursery – at first 180 in a box together for ten days. They eat a rich mixture of chalky earth and seaweed and are inclined to eat each other although this can be avoided by taking care that snails in one box are all of exactly the same age. It seems, however that sin has its reward because, if they do manage to find a comrade to eat, it advances the development of the successful cannibals by a fortnight. After ten days, during which time about twenty are lost, they are put into another box with only 80 snails, followed by a further ten days in a group of 40. During the month that they

Snails are happiest when it is warm and wet, which is why they come out after rain in the summer. To frustrate their tendency to go to sleep, M. Vadot keeps them in a steamy room which reproduces the humid conditions they like.

are in the nursery, they are kept awake by light and a perpetual temperature of 25°C and encouraged to eat so that they maintain a steady rate of growth. But if, as is the case with a few of them, they do not prosper, they are given a rest for a lunar month. The moon, we found, once again, is an important consideration in many branches of French agriculture.

At this stage the young snails are ready for what Jean-François calls the 'storm room', where they spend the next six to eight weeks. Snails like really bad weather. It is always after a heavy rainfall that wild snails come out, especially in summer when it is warm. In the ordinary course of nature, in dry weather and in the winter, snails spend much of their time sleeping and the stripes on their shells represent the interruption in their growth due to these periods of inactivity.

The 'storm room', still warm at 21°C and very humid, reproduces the dismal weather that snails appreciate, so they do not go to sleep. They live in tall cages, about 40,000 of them at any one time. Wherever a snail may be its tendency is always to climb, moving, by the way, at roughly 7.5 cm (3 in) a minute. In the nursery boxes they all cling to the lid. In the cages they climb to the top. The temperature in the storm room is so arranged that it is 2° cooler at the top of the cages than at the bottom. This encourages them to go back down to the bottom where their food is. They eat once a day in the evening, starting at about 6 pm and going on for six hours while the lights are on. Their diet here is slightly less rich and includes a certain amount of cereal, mostly maize and oats.

In between times they do not do very much. Jean-François has spent many long nights in the 'storm room', watching their behaviour: 'They just pass the whole night gossiping and dancing.' The result of this riotous living, with no sleep to impede their growth, is that they develop in three and a half months to the stage which would take a wild snail three years to achieve.

In the summer when it is warmer he can put some of the snails out of doors, but their rate of development is much slower. To equal the size of those in the 'storm room' they need twelve to fourteen weeks in the open air. At any one time, Jean-François may have 100,000 snails at all stages of development. In the course of a year he can hope to sell about 2 tons of snails.

His most prestigious customer is Bernard Loiseau, the famous chef who won his third Michelin star in 1991. The Côte d'Or at Saulieu became famous in the 1920s, when it was taken over by Alexandre Dumaine, one of the greatest chefs of this century. Loiseau moved there in 1975 and has gradually rebuilt its reputation, which had lapsed sadly since Dumaine's death. While Dumaine was a chef belonging very much in the traditional mould, Loiseau is a product of the modern Paul Bocuse stars-of-the-media style of cuisine. He is a man of infinite talent, but he has been driven on by the mistaken recent policy of the *Guide Michelin* of insisting on an absurd standard of luxury for the restaurants to which they award three stars. The third star means for a restaurateur probably a 60 per cent increase in turnover, but often he has to borrow so much money to make his establishment grand that, instead of a simple dedication to good food, the need for cash becomes the primary inspiration.

Loiseau is a restless, almost frenzied man, who is incapable of remaining in the same place for three minutes at a time. Delegation is obviously an exhausting struggle for him as he likes to be concerned with every minute aspect of the Côte d'Or, not just in the kitchen but in the hotel bedrooms and bathrooms. This passion for detail is wonderfully reflected in his cooking. He is the only first-class French chef to have devised a purely vegetarian set menu. It consists of eight courses of highly original dishes of all kinds of vegetables and reveals an unusual knowledge of the produce that goes into them. His vegetable supplier, Gérard Maternaud of Quarré les Tombes, maintains that he often learns something new during one of Loiseau's regular visits (see also the piece on vegetables).

There is nothing cranky about his interest in vegetables. He does not insist, for instance, on their being grown organically, only that they should grow naturally. In fact, M. Maternaud uses only cattle manure and eschews herbicides, incidentally having an amazing machine like a giant iron that puffs steam down into the soil,

Bernard Loiseau, who got his third Michelin star in 1992, likes to use snails, as he favours local produce, but he cooks them with nettles rather than the traditional garlic and parsley.

killing weeds to a depth of 10 cm (4 in).

It was his fondness for the natural that inspired Loiseau's snail dish. Obviously, being in Burgundy, he had to have snails on his menu. Rather than have the traditional, standard recipe, he decided to use stinging nettles instead of parsley. People pick these for him in the summer in the country around Saulieu and, he says, they freeze well.

With the snails themselves, he does not want the so-called Burgundy snail. The Gros Gris that Jean-François Vadot raises have a finer flesh, are paler and do not lose any weight in the cooking.

As a source of food there is a lot to be said for snails in general. In the wild, they eat mostly grass (approximately their own weight every day), and make a much better job of converting it into protein than, for example, cows which waste a lot of what they eat, turning it into bones and horns and fur and other irrelevant, inedible material. A snail has no skeleton, indeed nothing superfluous, except the shell it was born with.

This economical structure is also useful when it comes to cooking. The flesh of a snail has a porous quality so that it absorbs the butter and the flavour of any herb it is cooked with. The ease of cooking snails is immediately apparent from this recipe of Bernard Loiseau, whose singular talent is for making everyday materials taste rare and exceptional. His second recipe for wild rabbit is a further illustration of this.

La soupe d'escargots aux orties

SNAIL AND STINGING NETTLE SOUP

For 4

4 dozen snails
100 g (4 oz) stinging nettles (gather young tops
only, and wear gloves!)
2 carrots, peeled and chopped
2 large onions, peeled and pierced with a few
cloves
2 leeks, cleaned and chopped
1 *bouquet garni* (parsley, bay leaves)
juice of 1 lemon
salt and pepper

Put the carrots, onions, leeks and *bouquet garni* into a pan and cover with water. Simmer for 30 minutes. Remove the vegetables, discard the *bouquet garni* and cloves, and purée the vegetables in a blender.

Strip the nettles, wash, and blanch them in boiling water for 5 minutes. Drain and blend in their turn. Put aside.

Heat the snails in their juices and a little court-bouillon for about 10 minutes. Remove the shells. Put in 1 tablespoon of the puréed vegetables to thicken the sauce, then add the nettle purée. Season to taste with salt and pepper (nettles are naturally peppery), and add the juice of the lemon. Serve very hot in soup plates.

Le lapin de Garenne

WILD RABBIT WITH CABBAGE AND POTATO DUMPLINGS

For 4

2 saddles of wild rabbit
4 rabbit legs
500 ml (17 fl oz) dry white wine
a sprig of thyme
1-2 bay leaves
65 g (2½ oz) unsalted butter
2 tablespoons peanut oil
40 g (1½ oz) puréed onion
2 medium green leafy cabbages
salt and pepper
Crapiauds du Morvan (potato dumplings)
120 g (4½ oz) potatoes, boiled in their skins,
peeled and mashed
½ tablespoon *fromage blanc*
1 medium egg, beaten
½ tablespoon plain flour

The rabbit and sauce: Boil the wine to burn off the alcohol. Cool. Marinate the pieces of rabbit in this for 24 hours, with the herbs.

The next day, preheat the oven to 220-230°C(425-450°F) Gas 7-8. Take the pieces of rabbit out of the marinade and pat dry. In a deep frying pan, brown them in 20 g (¾ oz) of the butter and the peanut oil for 5 minutes on each side. Then put them in the preheated oven for 15 minutes to finish cooking. Put in a warm place in a heated serving dish. Reduce the oven to 160°C(325°F) Gas 3.

Pour off as much fat as possible from the frying pan and deglaze the meat juices by adding 200 ml (7 fl oz) of the white wine marinade; boil to reduce the sauce by half. Add 150 ml (5 fl oz) water and the onion purée. Bring to the boil for 2 minutes, and season with salt and pepper. Keep warm.

The cabbage: Cut away the outer green leaves and keep only the tender ones in the middle. Boil these for 3-4 minutes in salted water. Refresh, drain and shred.

The crapiauds du Morvan: In a bowl, mix the *fromage blanc* and half the egg only, then add the flour. Mix well again and add the potato. Season and divide into eight portions. Shape into ovals.

To serve: Heat the pieces of wild rabbit through in the warm oven, and the sauce in a pan. Heat the cooked shredded cabbage with 20 g (¾ oz) of the butter, and season to taste with salt and pepper. In a non-stick frying pan, heat the remaining butter and cook the potato dumplings for 1-2 minutes on each side. Drain on absorbent kitchen paper.

Arrange the rabbit pieces, cabbage and potato dumplings on a heated serving dish, and serve the sauce separately.

Bernard Loiseau

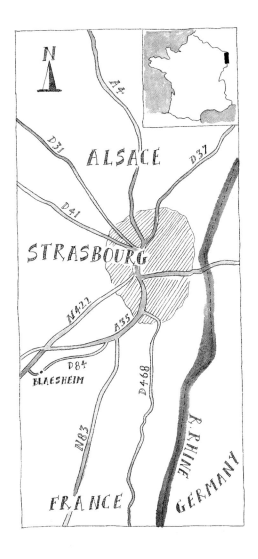

Choucroute

Thirty years ago or perhaps rather less, as one walked through the streets of Strasbourg in the early autumn, a pungent smell would assail one's nostrils – the unmistakable odour of fermenting *choucroute* rose from the depths of almost every house. Even today a few old grannies still insist on making their own at home, but for the most part this particularly Alsatian product is manufactured by much larger concerns. Certainly no restaurant makes its own.

I cannot say that I have ever much liked it, and the cabbage to the British is hardly a vegetable redolent of romance, but we decided that we must include *choucroute* because nearly every *brasserie* in the country, on account of the growing association with Alsace, serves *choucroute*. In fact, it was a happy decision, because our researches confirmed one of the themes of this book – that all products are at their best in their region of origin, where tradition has taught people how to get the most from whatever it is that prospers in their landscape. In Alsace, I came to see the point of *choucroute*.

To the north and the west lie beautiful forests, but the land immediately round Strasbourg is dull, often wrapped in bleak mists and fog. The villages with half-timbered houses have an unreal look, exaggerated by the more modern buildings, whose owners have a love of gnomes, miniature windmills, and fake storks' nests, complete with plastic stork droppings trailing down their roofs. The villages are surrounded by huge, flat fields with no hedges, and what the locals call a hill would not be noticed by even the feeblest of bicyclists.

Round Blaesheim, some 15 km (9 miles) from Strasbourg, these broad fields are filled with candlewick acres of cabbages, spread over the land for as far as one can

The cabbage that is used to make choucroute, *which is traditionally served in every French* brasserie, *is a species that came from China.*

see. The mayor of Blaesheim is Paul Baur, a bubbling 70–year–old, the President of the *choucroute* growers of France.

There was a time in the 1970s when the popularity of *choucroute* was dwindling and consumption was seriously down. M. Baur set about restoring the image of *choucroute*. 'We got up some recipes to convince people that it is not a heavy dish, old-fashioned and slow to prepare, but can be light and fit in with modern ways.'

After five minutes in his company, you begin to feel that you have been deceived all your life about cabbages. Instead of being something soggy, boiled to death in the vicarages of Britain, you now hear that they are rather exotic and foreign, and that the world has been a better place for their existence for 2,000 years or more.

There are various kinds of wild cabbage to be found on the shores of the Mediterranean and it is these that were developed for cultivation very early in Europe, but the type of cabbage best suited to make *choucroute* came from China. There is evidence that the workers who built the Great Wall of China in the third century BC had as one of their staples cabbage fermented in wine. How the dish came to Europe is open to question. The number of culinary notions that Marco Polo is supposed to have brought back with him inclines me to believe the other

The cabbage-grower tries to get each plant in a field to ripen at the same moment, because much of the picking is now done mechanically.

theory that it was brought in the thirteenth century by the Tartar hordes.

Paul Baur farms 85 hectares (212 acres) of which 30 hectares (75 acres) are devoted to cabbages. He plants about fifteen different varieties, all derived from *Brassica oleracea*, a big, round white-headed kind, rather beautiful in its spherical compactness. The seeds are planted in a nursery in the spring and two months later replanted in the fields. The soil here is deep and rich, watered by the river Ehn, which rises at the foot of Mont Ste Odile. Madame Baur attributes the astonishing fertility of the soil to these holy origins. Paul merely speaks of the primordial purity of the water. Whatever the case, the cabbages grow to a prodigious size – one single cabbage can weigh as much as 12-15 kg (26-33 lb).

The planting season lasts from mid-April until mid-June. Because the picking is now largely done mechanically, each group has to be certain to ripen at the same time. The first lot are ready to be picked in the last days of June. It takes a minimum of three weeks to make the cabbages into *choucroute*, so it is in time for the Quatorze Juillet that the first *choucroute* is ready to eat, and in these days of commercialism it is inevitably launched as *Choucroute Nouvelle*.

The process of manufacture is simple. The cabbages ride up a conveyor-belt

Ideally, the cabbages are ripe enough for picking in the last days of June so that the first choucroute *can be ready by the Quatorze Juillet.*

into a machine that strips them of their outer leaves and drills out the stalk and the core of the plant. Another machine then shreds the cabbage into fine strips, 7.5 cm (3 in) or so in length. Finally, the shredded plants are put into a large container with sea salt to 2 per cent of the total weight, which is to say not enough to act as a preservative but simply as a method of driving the liquid out of the cabbage. The shredded cabbage is then pressed firmly down and the container hermetically sealed to avoid any contact with the air.

Nothing else is added and nothing done. Without any kind of starter, a perfectly natural lactic fermentation happens and it was this that used to fill the streets of Strasbourg with its piercing smell. Old people say that they used to put wooden boards on the top of the cabbage and weigh it down with heavy stones. It was impossible to make the container truly airtight. Even in Paul's *choucrouterie* with the containers sealed with plastic sheets, rather as silage was until recently in Britain, streams of fermenting foam force their way from under the sealing sheets and the sharpened air catches at one's throat.

The fermentation lasts anything from two to eight weeks depending on the outside temperature, ideally 16°C to 18°C. In the heat of late summer, it is very

quick – 25°C is too high. Production goes on until the end of October when the cold weather starts.

As one goes round his *choucrouterie* with Paul Baur, he becomes more and more excited at the thought of making a convert to the wonders of his product. He can hardly bear to pass a container of *choucroute* without plunging his hand into it and giving one some to taste, as well as having a good mouthful himself. Besides the ordinary *choucroute*, although ordinary is not the apposite word for what he produces, he makes a small amount with shredded turnips, which is surprisingly delicious, but virtually unknown outside Alsace.

Alsace produces 75 per cent of all the *choucroute* made in France and 15 per cent comes from the small village of Blaesheim. There is naturally a measure of rivalry with Germany, where *sauerkraut*, after all, was the inspiration for one of their many nicknames.

There are also strict regulations in Germany, which the Alsatian producers hope will not become universal in the European Community. It is forbidden to wash *sauerkraut* after the fermentation, which leaves it with a more acid taste. It is also illegal to sell uncooked *sauerkraut*. This is a miserable regulation, as *choucroute* is particularly good raw in salads or the equivalent of a shrimp cocktail.

Paul waxes especially enthusiastic about the nutritional and eupeptic properties of *choucroute*. It was, he says, an English doctor who, in 1753, drew the attention of the Admiralty to the value of *choucroute* for sailors, so that all naval vessels were provided with large quantities before long voyages. It is one of the useful characteristics of *choucroute* that, reasonably sealed up against the air, it can stay fresh for a year. Captain Cook took dozens of barrels on his journeys of exploration as a prophylactic against scurvy and attributed the good health of his crews principally to *choucroute*. As well as brimming over with vitamin C, it is full of fibre to help the digestion, and is of benefit to diabetics.

As for the cooking, Paul says it should be cooked only briefly and that ready-cooked *choucroute* should be heated at a low heat, but for preference he likes it raw or lightly steamed. The most important thing is always to see that it is well drained.

The person Paul Baur has most confidence in as far as the preparation of his *choucroute* is concerned is François Lenhardt who owns the Maison des Tanneurs, a restaurant in the old quarter of Strasbourg known as Petite France. The houses are all timber-framed and lean at precarious angles, so that you feel you have strayed into a Walt Disney cartoon, for the effect is picturesque rather than beautiful. It is only when one examines the detail that these houses become really interesting – the

Fresh choucroute *is so different from* sauerkraut *as to be an unexpected treat. In Germany it is illegal to sell uncooked* sauerkraut*, whereas in France they realise that freshness is what gives* choucroute *its distinction.*

An Alsace choucroute, as cooked by chef François Lenhardt at Strasbourg's Maison des Tanneurs.

staircases, the doorways, the elaborate carving on the beams and pillars of the interiors reveal wonderful craftmanship.

The Maison des Tanneurs was built in 1572 as the headquarters of the Corporation of Tanners, with open spaces in the roof to allow the skins to dry. For many years it was a private house until François Lenhardt's maternal grandparents bought it in 1954 and started to run it as a restaurant. Inside, the restaurant echoes the quaintness of Petite France. The rooms are cluttered with every imaginable folksy object from dolls to china *chopes*, as the French call *steins*. The waiters wear long, red waistcoats with more brass buttons on them than I could count.

François, who is himself the chef, trained among other places at La Réserve at Beaulieu, but here his objective is to be as traditional as possible. He serves two dishes of the straightforward *choucroute* that all Alsatian families eat on festive occasions. The first is cooked with a local Riesling, the other with Crémant, which is to say with a sparkling wine made from a Pinot Blanc grape in the manner of Champagne. This version, he maintains is much lighter.

An orthodox *choucroute* comes with boiled bacon, various sausages, and pretty well anything else that comes to hand. To these he may add a *quenelle* or dumpling of chicken livers. Either of his *choucroutes* might have won over Elizabeth David, who politely excused all her readers from the obligation to do more than try it once. I found them excellent. Perhaps she was influenced by the German *sauerkraut*, which François Lenhardt says is too greasy and heavy with fruit.

Like Paul Baur, from whom he buys regular supplies of *choucroute* in 25 kg (55 lb) tubs, he reports an upsurge in the popularity of this Alsatian dish. Why, he says, is a mystery – 'unless it is simply that people want to get back to the authentic.'

Choucroute à l'Alsacienne

PICKLED WHITE CABBAGE ALSACE-STYLE

For 6

1.8 kg (4 lb) uncooked white *choucroute*
200 g (7 oz) onions, peeled and chopped
150 g (5 oz) goose fat (or butter)
500 ml (17 fl oz) Alsace white wine (Riesling)
12 medium potatoes, peeled
Seasonings and spices
3 garlic cloves, peeled
3 cloves
1 bay leaf
12 juniper berries
12 coriander seeds
12 white peppercorns
Meats
1 kg (2¼ lb) salted loin of pork
500 g (18 oz) smoked shoulder of pork
3 small hands of pork
300 g (11 oz) green bacon in one piece
300 g (11 oz) smoked bacon in one piece
6 Strasbourg sausages (*Knackwürste*)
6 small country-style frying sausages

Preheat the oven to 180-190°C(350-375°F) Gas 4-5.

Rinse the *choucroute* in cold water. Drain and press it dry.

Fry the onions gently in the goose fat until soft, then drain off the fat and reserve. Add the white wine to the onions, and mix with the *choucroute*.

Place all the pieces of pork and bacon on the bottom of a large casserole, and cover with the *choucroute*.

Make a 'bag' with a piece of gauze or muslin and wrap all the spices and seasonings in it. Place it in the middle of the pan, cover with the lid, heat, and when it comes to the boil, put in the preheated oven for 2 hours. Watch the liquid level carefully, and if necessary add a little more wine.

Half an hour before the *choucroute* is ready, remove the pieces of bacon from the casserole (keep warm), and put the peeled potatoes into the pan. Heat the *Knackwürste* in simmering water (don't boil them or they will split). Sauté the other sausages in a fry-ing pan with the reserved goose fat.

When the *choucroute* is ready, still slightly crunchy, take the remaining meats out of the pan. Check the seasoning.

Place the *choucroute* in a warm serving dish. Cut the meats in portions, except for the hands of pork which you want to display whole on top of the *choucroute*. Place the pieces of meat and the sausages around it. Serve hot with the potatoes as accompaniment.

Tarte à l'oignon

ONION TART

For 6

250 g (9 oz) shortcut pastry
500 g (18 oz) onions, peeled and finely sliced
50 g (2 oz) butter
50 g (2 oz) plain flour
100 ml (3½ fl oz) *crème fraîche*
100 ml (3½ fl oz) milk
3 egg yolks
150 g (5 oz) smoked bacon, diced
a pinch of grated nutmeg
salt and pepper

Preheat the oven to 220°C(425°F) Gas 7.

Brown the onions gently in the butter in a non-stick pan. Sprinkle the flour on to the onions, then add the *crème fraîche* and milk. Season with nutmeg, salt and pepper, then simmer for 10 minutes, stirring frequently.

When the onions are cooked, mix in the egg yolks off the heat and reserve on one side to cool.

Blanch the bacon in water (starting in cold water), then drain carefully. Dry fry in a frying pan until crisp (discard the fat).

Roll out the pastry and use to line a tart tin of at least 25 cm (10 in) in diameter. Pour in the onion mixture and sprinkle the lardons on top. Bake in the preheated oven for 25 minutes.

François Lenhardt

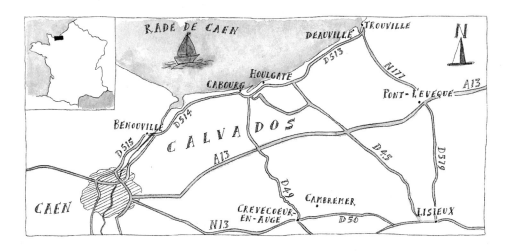

Apples

In gastronomy at any rate, Normandy and the apple are practically synonymous. Le Pays d'Auge, the home of one of the two *appellations contrôlées* to do with Calvados (the one that is distilled twice, like Cognac), has given its name to many dishes involving apples. Its orchards were the pride of the region. Unfortunately the last 30 years have seen a sorry decline in both the number and the quality of the orchards of Normandy.

The traditional way of planting an orchard was with the trees well spaced and so pruned that the lowest branches were above the reach of the cattle that grazed beneath them. The cattle, naturally, fertilised the soil. In the department of the Manche, for instance, three million of these trees have disappeared for various reasons. Many were torn up when their owners switched to other crops, a blight carried off many more and the hurricane of 1987 blew down thousands, although in this case it was mostly old, enfeebled trees that suffered.

The old method of planting means a delay of anything from ten to fifteen years before the trees bear any reasonable amount of fruit. It is not surprising that many growers adopt more commercial methods, planting the trees more densely and not cutting off the lower branches. They fence them in, not allowing cattle anywhere near them. This means that the new trees may well fruit in only three years.

The apples are nothing like as good. Furthermore, the temptation to plant marketable varieties like La Golden (Golden Atrocious) is overwhelming.

The question of varieties is a gloomy one. A great many have disappeared

Except for the making of Calvados, there is far less interest today in the variety of applies that used to grow in Normandy. Few fruit farmers grow more than ten different varieties; many have been lost altogether. Overleaf: The art of grafting has largely died out in the last 40 years. Happily there is now a movement towards arousing public interest in saving old varieties and skills.

altogether since the last war. The Pays d'Auge claims still to have 150 different varieties in its district, but it is difficult to be sure. One village may have a variety unknown in the next, but the same apple may go by a different name a few miles away. Only about 40 different kinds are now used in cider-making. Most Augeron fruit farmers could name twenty or so varieties, but few grow as many as ten kinds.

The Schlumberger Foundation, which owns the Château de Crèvecoeur-en-Auge, is making a splendid attempt to reverse the trend to uniformity. By way of an example, it has planted in the castle orchard some 30 traditional varieties – with lovely names such as Pomme de Beurre, Bon Père, Belle Fleur Jaune, Claque Pépin, Court-pendu and Reinette d'Armorique – that were in danger of being lost forever.

The Foundation mounts exhibitions on the care of trees, demonstrations of the art of grafting (which has died out in the last 40 years), and lectures on the diseases of apple trees. It tries to promote public interest in the preservation of a great

tradition. Nevertheless, it is something of a lone voice, crying out against the claims of mediocrity.

The apple story is not much happier in the realm of cuisine. The Manoir d'Hastings is a delightful hotel, in Bénouville, just north-east of Caen. The main building, which holds the restaurant, is a seventeenth-century manor house, simply furnished in good taste. To one side is a modern block with a small orchard in front of it. A most amicable young couple, José and Carole Aparicio have recently bought the place, but I got no feeling that the orchard played any other than a decorative role, either under the old regime or the new one.

José, a first-class chef, is as keen as any other young man of today to use local produce, and he does a lot with apples. Coming from Périgord, he is fond of *foie gras* which, oddly enough, is a burgeoning new product in Calvados. He finds that it blends well with apples. Apples feature largely in his desserts, including a charlotte, a soufflé and a *gratin de pommes*. He uses Calvados in many dishes and *Pommeau* (see below) in a particularly good scallop dish.

When I came to talk to him about varieties, he did not have a great deal to say. 'In my cooking, I use Golden and Boscop. Golden hold together much better, but the taste is rather bland. Boscop has a much better taste, but does not keep so firm.'

I like to think that as serious a chef as José will, when he has been longer in the region, investigate the possible alternatives more energetically. If he doesn't, nobody else will. In all the local recipe books I consulted hardly any ever mentioned the variety of apple to be used except for an occasional vague reference to Reinette. Few of the chefs of Normandy deal with a particular grower of apples, but buy them from wholesalers.

It is, I feel, something of a cautionary tale. The apple has lost the battle with the marketeer and the ignorant consumer. Let us hope the other ingredients in this book may be saved from a similar fate.

Pigeonneau poêlé au cidre

BABY PIGEONS IN CIDER

For 4

4 baby pigeons
2 tablespoons raisins
1 bottle of cider
100 g (4 oz) butter
75 ml (2½ fl oz) Calvados
4 apples, cored and cut into wedges
250 ml (8 fl oz) reduced meat stock
salt and pepper

The day before: Ask the butcher to clean the birds. Burn off the down remaining on the skin with a flame, and bone the pigeons, except for the legs and wings, cutting the breasts carefully off the carcass. Keep the pigeon in a cool place.

Soak the raisins in 250 ml (8 fl oz) of the cider.

To cook: Preheat the oven to 220°C(425°F) Gas 7.

Season the birds. In a casserole, lightly brown 50 g (2 oz) of the butter, and fry the pigeons for 5 minutes. Pour in the cider and raisins, cover, and cook in the preheated oven for 15 minutes. The meat must remain pink.

Take the birds out of the oven, and *flambé* with the Calvados. Deglaze with a dash of cider and add the apple wedges and stock. Bring to the boil and take the pan off the heat.

Place the pigeons and apple wedges on serving plates. Beat the remaining butter into the sauce and coat the pigeons with it.

Coquilles St-Jacques au pistil de safran et pâtes fraîches

SCALLOPS IN SAFFRON SAUCE WITH FRESH PASTA

For 6

24 large scallops, removed from shells
300 g (11 oz) fresh pasta
100 g (4 oz) butter
200 ml (7 fl oz) double cream
50 ml (2 fl oz) *Pommeau* (or cider or apple brandy)
a pinch of saffron threads, infused in a little boiling water
salt and pepper

Cook the pasta in boiling salted water until *al dente,* timing according to type. Drain well.

Trim the scallops, cut them in half and pat dry. Fry them lightly in the butter for a minute or so. Add the cream and alcohol, and season to taste with salt and pepper.

On each warm plate, arrange a bed of pasta. Remove the scallops with a slotted spoon and arrange around the pasta bed. Strain the sauce into another pan and add the saffron. Stir, then coat the plates with the sauce.

José Aparicio

Pommeau is a mixture of freshly squeezed apple juice and *eau de vie de cidre* (a rougher version of apple brandy than Calvados).

Gazetteer

LAMB

Chef: Olivier Roellinger

Restaurant: Maison de Bricourt,
1 rue Daguesclin,
35260 Cancale
Tel: 99 89 64 76

Suppliers: Yves Fantou,
St-Broladre
Tel: 99 80 25 47

Raymond Boyer,
Les Coulayes,
14160 L'Escale,
Provence

OYSTERS

Chef: Patrice Caillault

Restaurant: Domaine du Château
de Rochevilaine,
Pointe de Pen-Lan,
Muzillac,
56190 Billiers
Tel: 97 41 61 61

Supplier: Michel Haumont,
St Armel,
Golfe de Morbihan

EELS

Chef: Charles Barrier

Restaurant: Restaurant
Charles Barrier,
101 avenue de la
Tranchée,
37021 Tours,
Indre-et-Loire
Tel: 47 54 20 39

Supplier: M. et Mme Baudray,
44310 Passay

MUSHROOMS

Chef: Christian Ravinel

Restaurant: Le Moulin de l'Abbaye,
24310 Brantôme en
Périgord
Tel: 53 05 80 22

Supplier: René Naboulet,
St Marie de Chignac

FOIE GRAS

Chef: Mme Gracia

Restaurant: La Belle Gasconne,
47170 Poudenas
Tel: 53 65 71 58

Supplier: Alain Cescalti,
Haous,
47170 Mézin

BREBIS CHEESE

Chef: Pascal Arcé

Restaurant: Arcé,
64430 St-Etienne-de-
Baïgorry
Tel: 59 37 40 14

Supplier: Raymond (Eramoun)
Marticorena,
'Maison Otsobia',
64430 St-Etienne-de-
Baïgorry

ARMAGNAC

Chef: André Daguin

Restaurant: Hôtel de France,
Place de la Libération,
32000 Auch
Tel: 62 05 00 44

Suppliers: Paul Dubourdieu,
Domaine de Broustet,
47170 Lannes,
Mézin

La Maison Marcel
Trépout,
Monastère Notre-
Dame,
Vic-Fezensac, Gers
Tel: 62 06 33 83

Jacques Théaux,
Domaine de Sans,
Cazeneuve,
32800 Eauze
Tel: 62 09 90 36

CANTAL CHEESE

Chefs: M. et Mme André Combourieu

Restaurant: Auberge des Montagnes, Pailherols, 15800 Vic-sur-Cère Tel: 71 47 57 01

Supplier: Jules Porte, 15800 Raulhac, Cantal

BEEF

Chef: Michel Bras

Restaurant: Michel Bras, Route d'Aubrac, 12210 Laguiole Tel: 65 44 32 24

Suppliers: Lucien Conquet, 12110 Laguiole Tel: 65 44 33 05

Paul Mathieu, Lhon, Laguiole

TRUFFLES

Chef: Alain Pic

Restaurant: Pic, 285 avenue Victor Hugo, 26001 Valence Tel: 75 44 15 32

Supplier: Pierre Aymé, Qua Bramarels, 26230 Grignan

VEGETABLES

Chef: Bernard Loiseau

Restaurant: La Côte d'Or, 2 rue d'Argentine, 21210 Saulieu, Côte d'Or, Bourgogne Tel: 80 64 07 66

Suppliers: Jean-Luc Daneyrolles, La Molière, Saignon, Apt Tel: 90 74 44 68

Gérard Maternaud, Les Guichards, 89630 Quarré-les-Tombes, Yonne, Bourgogne Tel: 86 32 20 94

OLIVE OIL

Chefs: Pierre et Jany Gleize

Restaurant: La Bonne Etape, 04160 Château-Arnoux Tel: 92 64 00 09

Supplier: Julien Masse, Moulin de la Cascade, Route de la Sigeuve, 04700 Lurs

PIGEONS

Chef: Alain Ducasse

Restaurant: Louis XV, Hôtel de Paris, Place Casino, Monte Carlo, Monaco Tel: 93 50 80 80

Supplier: Claire Dillard, Le Haut Serre, Valavoire, 04250 La Motte-du-Caire

FROGS

Chef: Philippe Jousse

Restaurant: Alain Chapel, 01390 Mionnay Tel: 78 91 82 02

Supplier: René Maisson, Ambérieu-en-Bugey Tel: 74 00 84 92

POULETS DE BRESSE

Chef: Georges Blanc

Restaurant: Georges Blanc,
01540 Vonnas,
Tel: 74 50 00 10

Suppliers: Daniel Blanc,
La Varna,
01560 Curciat-
Dongalon

Les Volailles Miéral,
Rue Bresse-Cocagne,
10340 Montrevel-en-
Bresse

Gilbert Billoud,
'Montalapiat',
01560 Curciat-
Dongalon
Tel: 74 52 92 08

CHAR

Chef: Charles Plumex,

Restaurant: Le Prieuré,
68 Grande Rue,
74200 Thonon-les-
Bains
Tel: 50 71 31 89

Supplier: Pierre Portier,
Route de Lavoret,
74200 Anthy sur
Léman
Tel: 50 70 31 99

SANCERRE

Chefs: M. et Mme Daniel
Fournier

Restaurant: Restaurant de la Tour,
Place de la Halle,
18300 Sancerre
Tel: 48 54 00 81

Suppliers: Alphonse Mellot,
Sancerre

Francis Cottat,
Chavignol

SNAILS

Chef: Bernard Loiseau

Restaurant: La Côte d'Or,
2 rue d'Argentine,
21201 Saulieu
Tel: 80 64 07 66

Supplier: Jean-François Vadot,
21320 Blancey
Tel: 80 64 64 75

CHOUCROUTE

Chef: François Lenhardt

Restaurant: Maison des Tanneurs,
42 rue de Bain aux
Plantes,
67000 Strasbourg
Tel: 88 32 79 70

Supplier: Paul Baur,
67113 Blaesheim
Tel: 88 68 88 39

APPLES

Chef: José Aparicio,

Restaurant: Le Manoir d'Hastings,
14970 Bénouville
Tel: 31 44 62 43

Supplier: Schlumberger
Foundation,
Château de
Crèvecoeur-en-Auge,
14340 Cambremer
Tel: 31 63 02 45

Index

Page numbers in *italic* refer to the illustrations

Alsace, 140-6
Aparicio, Carole, 152
Aparicio, José, 152
apples, 148-53, *149-51*
    pigeonneau poêlé au cidre, 153
Apt, 80-4
Arce, Pascal, 45-6
Armagnac, 50-7, *53, 55*
    la glace aux pruneaux à l'Armagnac, 57
Aymé, Pierre, 74, *75-7, 77*
asparagus: *velouté d'asperges aux pointes d'asperges*, 85
    l'assiette de fromage de brebis au membrillo, 43
aubergines: *charlotte de dorade aux aubergines*, 79
    noisettes d'agneau au thym, courgettes et aubergines, 91
Aubrac cattle, 65, *65, 68-71, 68, 69*
Auvergne, 58-62, *66-7*

Baïgorry, 44-8
Barrier, Charles, 9, 28-30
Basques, 45-8
Baudray, André, 24, 25, 26-8, *27*, 30
Baur, Paul, 141-5, 146
la bavette poêlée sur un jus aux céréeales fermentées, graines germées, 72
beef, 64-73, *65*
    la bavette poêlée sur un jus aux céréeales fermentées, graines germées, 72
Billoud, Gilbert, *109*, 112
Blaesheim, 140-1, 145
Blanc, Daniel, 110-12
Blanc, Georges, 113-14
Blancey, 132-3
Blonde d'Aquitaine cattle, 64, 71
Bocuse, Paul, 9-10, 95, 114, 137
Boyer, Raymond, 12-13, 15

brandy, Armagnac, 50-6
Brantôme, 33-6
Bras, Michel, 71, 80
bream: *charlotte de dorade aux aubergines*, 79
brebis cheese, 44-9, *48*
Bresse, 108-14
Brillat-Savarin, 108, 113
Bué, 129
Burgundy, 132-8

cabbage: *choucroute*, 140-7, *141-6*
    choucroute à l'Alsacienne, 147
    le lapin de Garenne, 139
Caillault, Patrice, 20-1
Calvados, 152
Cantal cheese, 58-63, *60-1*
    salade Cantalouse, 63
    tourtes au Cantal, 63
cattle, 64-73, *65, 68, 69*
cèpes, 32-3, 36
    charlotte de canard confit aux cèpes, 37
    rocamadour rôti aux cèpes, 37
    salade de cèpes au mesclun, 91
Cescalti, Alain, 40-2, *40*
Chapel, Alain, 96, 102, 106
char, 116-23, *117-21*
    omble-chevalier au vin jaune et à la coriandre, 123
charlotte de canard confit aux cèpes, 37
charlotte de dorade aux aubergines, 79
Charolais cattle, 64-5, 133
cheese: *l'assiette de fromage de brebis au membrillo*, 43
    brebis cheese, 44-9, *48*
    Cantal cheese, 58-63, *60-1*
    crottin de Chavignol, 127-8
    rocamadour rôti aux cèpes, 37
    salade Cantalouse, 63
    tourtes au Cantal, 63
chicken: *coq fermier au Sancerre blanc*, 131
    poularde de Bresse à la crème façon grand-mère Blanc, 114-15
    poulets de Bresse, 108-15, *109, 111, 113*
    see also liver
choucroute, 140-7, *141-6*
choucroute à l'Alsacienne, 147
cider: *pigeonneau poêlé au cidre*, 153

cod, salt *see* salt cod
Combourieu, André, 61-2
Combourieu, Jean, 62
Compagnie Polder, 14-15, *15*
Conquet, Lucien, 64-5, 71
coq fermier au Sancerre blanc, 131
coquilles St-Jacques au pistil de safran et pâtes fraîches, 153
Côte du Rhône, 74
Cottat, Francis, 127-9, *127*
courgettes: *noisettes d'agneau au thym, courgettes et aubergines*, 91
crayfish: *gâteau de foies blonds de poulardes de bresse, sauce aux écrevisses et truffes*, 107
Crèvecoeur-en-Auge, Château de, *149*
cromesquis d'huîtres aux poireaux, 23
crottin de Chavignol, 127-8

Daguin, André, *54*, 55, 56
Daneyrolles, Jean-Luc, 80-4, *81-3*
David, Elizabeth, 146
Dillard, Claire, 8, 92-5, *93, 94*, 97
La Dombes, 100-6, *101*, 109
dried fruit: *farcement de Bernex à la façon de Haute-Savoie*, 123
Dubourdieu, Paul, 53-5, *53, 56*
Ducasse, Alain, 95-7, *97*
duck: *charlotte de canard confit aux cèpes*, 37
    see also foie gras
Dumaine, Alexandre, 137
dumplings: *le lapin de Garenne*, 139

eels, 24-31, *25*
    matelote d'anguilles au Bourgueil, 30
    terrine de poisson, 31
eggs: *oeufs pochés au Sancerre rouge*, 131
ewe's milk, 45-6
    le pot de caillé de brebis ou mamilla, 43

Fantou, Yves, 15-16

*farcement de Bernex à la façon de
Haute-Savoie*, 123
fish: char, 116-23, *117-21*
terrine de poisson, 31
Floc de Gascogne, 54-5
foie de canard frais à la julienne,
57
foie gras, 38-43, *40-1*
*foie de canard frais à la
julienne*, 57
*poitrine de pigonneau de nid
avec foie gras de canard
grillé*, 98
salade de l'auberge, 43
*tartine de foie gras au Floc de
Gascogne*, 43
Fournier, Daniel, 129-30
frogs, 100-7, *103-5*
*pommes de terre farcies aux
truffes blanches, cuisses de
grenouilles à la ciboulette*,
106
fruit: *les fruit rouges, semoule et
crème glacée à la reine des
prés*, 73

Gascony, 50-6
*gâteau de foies blonds de
poulardes de bresse, sauce
aux écrevisses et truffes*, 107
*la glace aux pruneaux à
l'Armagnac*, 57
Gleize, Jany, 8, 11, *11*, 86-8,
90
Gleize, Pierre, 8, 11, *11*, 12,
16, 78, 80, 86-8, 90
goats' cheese, 127-8
goose: *foie gras*, 39-42, *41*
Gracia, Madame, 38-40
Grand-Lieu, Lac de, 24-5, *29*,
30
grapes, Armagnac, 52
Grignan, 74
Guérard, Michel, 95-6
Guerlain, M., 24-5

haricot beans: *morue de Bilbao
rôtie et haricots blancs*, 99
Haumont, Michel, 18-20, *19*
Hippocrates, 90

ice cream: *les fruits rouges,
semoule et crème glacée à la
reine des prés*, 73
la glace aux pruneaux à

l'Armagnac, 57

Jousse, Philippe, 102, 106
junket: *le pot de caillé de brebis
ou mamilla*, 43

Laguiole, 70-1
lamb, 12-17
*noisettes d'agneau au thym,
courgettes et aubergines*, 91
*rond de selle d'agneau de pré-
salé du Mont St Michel*, 17
see also sweetbreads
le lapin de Garenne, 139
leeks: *cromesquis d'huîtres aux
poireaux*, 23
Léman, Lac, 116-21
Lenhardt, François, 145-6
lettuce: *salade de cèpes au
mesclun*, 91
Limousin cattle, 64
liver: *gâteau de foies blonds de
poulardes de bresse, sauce
aux écrevisses et truffes*, 107
lobsters: *petits homards aux
saveurs de l'Ile aux épices*,
17
Loiseau, Bernard, 64, 80, 84,
137-8, *138*

La Maison Marcel Trépout,
55
Maisson, René, 102-6, *103*,
105
Manfredi, Paola, 26, 28
Marticorena, Raymond
(Eramoun), 46-8, *47*
Masse, Julien, *87-9*, 88-90
*matelote d'anguilles au
Bourgueil*, 30
Maternaud, Gérard, 84, 137-8
Mathieu, Paul, 65-70, *65*, 71
meadowsweet ice cream, 73
Les Mées, 86-8
Mellot, Alphonse, 126-7, *127*,
128, 129
Mellot, Joseph, 126
Meneau, Marc, 80, 84
Miéral, Jean-Claude, 112
Monselet, 78
Mont St Michel, 13, *13*
*Morue de Bilbao rôtie et haricots
blancs*, 99
Morvan, 84
mushrooms, 32-7, *33*

*charlotte de canard confit aux
cèpes*, 37
rocamadour rôti aux cèpes, 37
salade de cèpes au mesclun, 91

Naboulet, René, 34-6, *35*
nettles: *la soupe d'escargots aux
orties*, 139
*noisettes d'agneau au thym,
courgettes et aubergines*, 91
Normandy, 148-52
Notre-Dame des Dombes,
102

oeufs pochés au Sancerre rouge,
131
olive oil, 86-91, *87-90*
*ombre-chevalier au vin jaune et à
la coriandre*, 123
onions: *tarte à l'oignon*, 147
oysters, 18-23, *19*, *20*, *22*
*cromesquis d'huîtres aux
poireaux*, 23
petits feuilletés d'huîtres au
seigle, 23

pasta: *coquilles St-Jacques au
pistil de safran et pâtes
fraîches*, 153
Le Pays d'Auge, 148-52
peppers: *poivrons farcis*, 115
Périgord, 33-6, *33*, 74-5, 129,
152
*petits feuilletés d'huîtres au
seigle*, 23
*petits homards aux saveurs de
l'Ile aux epices*, 17
Pic, Alain 78
Pic, Jacques, 9, 77-8
pies: *tourtes au Cantal*, 63
pigeonneau poêlé au cidre, 153
pigeons, 92-9, *93-5*
pigeonneau poêlé au cidre, 153
*poitrine de pigonneau de nid
avec foie gras de canard
grillé*, 98
Pliny, 75, 90
Plumex, Charles, 121-2
Point, Fernand, 9
*poitrine de pigonneau de nid avec
foie gras de canard grillé*, 98
poivrons farcis, 115
*Pommeau: coquilles St-Jacques
au pistil de safran et pâtes
fraîches*, 153

pommes de terre farcies aux truffes blanches, cuisses de grenouilles à la ciboulette, 106
Porte, Jules, 58-61, *59-61,* 62
Portier, Pierre, 116-21, *117-19*
le pot de caillé de brebis ou mamilla, 43
potatoes: *farcement de Bernex à la façon de Haute-Savoie,* 123
le lapin de Garenne, 139
pommes de terre farcies aux truffes blanches, cuisses de grenouilles à la ciboulette, 106
truffes de la drôme en cocotte de pomme de terre, 79
Poudenas, 38-9
poularde de Bresse à la crème façon grand-mère Blanc, 114-15
poulets de Bresse, 108-15, *109, 111, 113*
pré-salé sheep, 12-16, *13, 16*
Provence, 86-90, 92-5
prunes: *la glace aux pruneaux à l'Armagnac,* 57
Pyrenees, 44-8, *45*

quince paste: *l'assiette de fromage de brebis au membrillo,* 43

rabbit: *le lapin de Garenne,* 139
ragoût de légumes, 85
Ravinel, Christian, 34, 36

les ris d'agneau sautés aux échalottes, 43
rocamadour rôti aux cèpes, 37
Roellinger, Olivier, 13-14, 15, 16
rond de selle d'agneau de pré-salé du Mont St Michel, 17

saffron: *coquilles St-Jacques au pistil de safran et pâtes fraîches,* 153
salads: *salade Cantalouse,* 63
salade de cèpes au mesclun, 91
salade de l'auberge, 43
Salers cattle, 58-9, *59,* 65, 69
salt cod: *morue de Bilbao rôtie et haricots blancs,* 99
Sancerre, 124-31, *125, 126, 128*
sauerkraut, 145
Savoyard potato and dried fruit gratin, 123
scallops: *coquilles St-Jacques au pistil de safran et pâtes fraîches,* 153
Schlumberger Foundation, 149-52
semolina: *les fruits rouges, semoule et crème glacée à la reine des prés,* 73
sheep, 12-16, *13, 16*
sheep's cheese, 46-8
snails, 132-9, *133-6, 138*
la soupe d'escargots aux orties, 139
soups: *la soupe d'escargots aux orties,* 139
velouté d'asperges aux pointes

d'asperges, 85
Strasbourg, 140, 143, 145-6
sweetbreads: *les ris d'agneau sautés aux échalottes,* 43

tarte à l'oignon, 147
tartine de foie gras au Floc de Gascogne, 43
terrine de poisson, 31
Théaux, Jacques, 55-6
Thuilier, Raymond, 9
tourtes au Cantal, 63
truffles, 74-9, *77, 78*
gâteau de foies blonds de poulardes de bresse, sauce aux écrevisses et truffes, 107
pommes de terre farcies aux truffes blanches, cuisses de grenouilles à la ciboulette, 106
truffes de la drôme en cocotte de pomme de terre, 79

Vadot, Jean-François, 133-7, *133, 136,* 138
Vaucluse, 80
vegetables, 80-5, *81-3*
ragoût de légumes, 85
velouté d'asperges aux pointes d'asperges, 85
Vergé, Roger, 96

wine, Sancerre, 124-31, *126, 128*
coq fermier au Sancerre blanc, 131
oeufs pochés au Sancerre rouge 131

Acknowledgements

Quentin Crewe, John Brunton and Ebury Press would like to thank Marie Christine Dargent and Colette Martin for their help in the production of this book.

All photography in the book was shot on Velvia professional film, kindly provided by Fuji Film France. John Brunton uses Canon cameras.